Orchids in the Shadows

Between Darkness and Light in Cuba

From the author of
Waiting on Zapote Street,
winner of the Latino Books Into Movies
Award, Drama TV Series category
and
Brothers: The Pedro Pan Boys
Winner of the International Latino Books
Awards, Best Fiction Novel category

Betty Viamontes

Orchids in the Shadows

Between Darkness and Light in Cuba

Published in the United States by

Zapote Street Books, LLC, Tampa, Florida

Book cover by SusanasBooks LLC

This book contains elements of fiction and creative non-fiction.

ISBN: 979-1-955848-21-3

Printed in the United States of America

I dedicate this book to—

The Cuban families on the island struggling to survive, fighting between darkness and light, and holding onto their faith in God and the hope for a better future.

My mother for showing me that anything is possible.

My beloved husband and my family for all their support.

My loyal readers, for reading my books and encouraging me to keep writing.

The members of all the book clubs who have so kindly chosen to read *Waiting on Zapote Street*, *The Dance of the Rose*, *Candela's Secrets and Other Havana Stories*, *Havana: A Son's Journey Home*, and *The Girl from White Creek* for group discussions.

To Facebook groups: All Things Cuban for providing a space to share stories and the culture of the Cuban people, and *Women Reading Great* Books for creating a forum for authors and readers to meet.

Foreword

Betty Viamontes has dedicated over twenty years of her life to documenting the lives of Cuban exiles. This time, however, her writing takes her to a small religious town in Cuba, one that has been slowly disappearing.

Her narration is purposely simple, but the issues she exposes are complex. The cast of characters introduced in the chapters illustrates various aspects of life in Remedios. But in a small town like this one, tarnished by hardship and a bleak economic reality, making connections is as important as breathing.

The small town of San Juan de los Remedios, known as Remedios, is a place of ghosts and legends, of churchgoing people clinging to faith as a castaway on the shore of hope. Their resilience is often tested.

Betty bases their stories on true events, on the lives of families that reside in this town. Within the reality of these stories, elements of fiction evolve to intrigue and engage the reader, while maintaining an accurate historical context.

Life for its main character, Amelia, is by any definition boring. An attorney by education, she has no other option but to work at a church. Why would an attorney work at a church? Betty explores the reasons and the need to conform to the incomprehensible.

Foreword

However, everything changes when a stranger, Frank, comes to town. The Miami, Florida, resident is seeking individuals who may have known his mother. Amelia connects him with his past, and both their lives change in ways they never anticipated.

As each character is introduced, their mutual connection is not immediately apparent. However, each character is linked to the other in aspects they will discover. These ties might be the key to their survival.

Written by Susana Jiménez-Mueller
Author of *Now I Swim*
Co-author of *Flight of the Tocororo*
Author and producer of *The Green Plantain –
The Cuban Stories Project podcast*

Chapter 1

San Juan Bautista de los Remedios

(The church)

Since 1548, I have stood in the town of Remedios, bearing witness to it all—from grieving parents to children whose faces glow with the promise of a better future.

My orange-and-white façade announces my presence across from the main square, lined with cafés, an ATM, a cigar shop, and a small market. Tourists often come. Their guides speak of my history, my architecture, and my original wood carvings, gilded in gold.

For centuries, I have watched thousands of baptisms and weddings, and heard just as many sermons for the departed. Weddings have changed over time—from the sumptuous gowns of decades past to today's simple dresses, sewn at home or passed down through generations.

Everything is different, yet the same.

Fewer coins fall into my donation box now. I have welcomed many notable visitors, including the island's president—though he is not received with the same warmth as others. The townspeople's quiet resentment has emptied familiar faces from my benches.

It saddens me to see so many young people leave, weary of waiting for change. Those who remain fill my halls with heavier prayers.

"God, I pray my daughter makes it safely to the United States," a mother once whispered.

For six months, she came daily, sitting on the same wooden bench, her prayers unwavering. Then, one day, she stopped.

Word spread that her daughter had died in the Darién jungle.

They told the grieving mother her child was in a better place—that she was finally free. The family held a service in her honor. The entire town came to mourn. And then, as it always does, life went on.

Recently, I have been restored—made beautiful again, if I may say so. I only wish the townspeople could do the same for their homes.

"The government controls all the repair materials," a parishioner once whispered. "And what's sold on the black market, we cannot afford."

I heard a man tell a priest that part of his ceiling had collapsed, nearly killing his grandmother in the kitchen. The priest listened with compassion. But his duty is to guide souls toward God. And here, it is becoming easier to lose one's faith.

My purpose is to help them hold on to it.

I stand just three miles from the northern coast, at the heart of the island—a pillar of faith amid deepening despair. The priests and nuns do what they can for their parishioners, but they cannot provide food or medicine, nor can they enter politics. They must remain neutral, even when neutrality feels like silence.

God knows that if people lose their faith, they will have lost everything.

And so I remain—if these walls do not crumble under the weight of sorrow—offering what comfort I can, a place to rest, a space for prayer, and bearing witness to the slow unraveling of a nation that refuses to die.

Chapter 2

The Blackout

(Amelia)

Every day is a race against the blackout. We know it will arrive, but not when. And when it does, the heat will grow, that heat that melts sidewalks and our very souls.

When darkness comes, I rush to light the candle I left on top of the square dining-room table, a table not big enough for the seven people who live in our house: my mother and uncle, my two nieces and their parents, and me. Then we sit around the table.

"Mami, Tío, do you want me to splash some water on your face?" I ask my mother and my uncle, who walk aided by metal walkers.

"Maybe a little later," she responds. "Stay here now."

"Tía Amelia, tell me a ghost story," my six-year-old niece says.

Her father shakes her head, but after my niece's insistence, I shrug and tell her about some of the haunted houses in Remedios, stories that are passed from generation to generation.

Amelia. That's what my mother named me, which in Hebrew means "work of God" and in

4

Germanic connotes fertility and industriousness. Some might say I do the work of God when I organize activities for a group of teenagers at church and for other people's children. But I will never have children or get married. Helping others' children will have to do.

From the day of my birth, on March 15, 1977, forty-five years ago, I seemed predestined to live in darkness. Yet I bring light into my life by stepping into the faded splendor of an old church in the town of Remedios—in the province of Villa Clara, Cuba— a town of legends, ghosts, parranda, and pirates.

I feel at peace when I enter the church, and my footsteps echo on the tiled floors. The walls protect me from the outside world, from the soldiers that monitor the square. The saints inside it bear witness to my prayers. They stand tall, offering comfort.

"God, we pray a miracle. Please save us from the ruthless and the godless. Give the people in this town hope."

After speaking with God and making the sign of the cross, I step into a small office where my responsibilities await. Using the old computer, which sits on a cluttered desk, I record each birth, death, and wedding.

Josefa Rodríguez Pérez was born on the 15th of September 2022 in the town of Remedios to her parents, Antonio Rodríguez Coto and Leila Pérez Fernandez. This is one of many entries. But over the past 20 years, the population has declined by more than 25%.

Currently, fewer than 34,000 people live here. The average age is forty-two. Ten of Remedios's inhabitants are over one hundred years old. Somehow, they have managed to survive. They have seen it all: such a blessing and a curse to live that long.

I enjoy talking to Teresa, one of the oldest women in town, whose mind remains intact. Teresa remembers better times when it wasn't necessary to form long lines, when milk wasn't restricted by age, and when a slice of cheese wasn't a luxury.

Teresa can no longer make long lines to buy her monthly quota, but some of us take turns helping her. My mother says some angels still walk among us.

Watching the town's population decline makes me wonder if, one day, Remedios will cease to exist. But I cannot worry about such things. More pressing and immediate problems trouble me.

I don't make much money, despite being an attorney by education. The church is the only employer that hires a blacklisted person like me, so this will be my job for as long as I live: recordkeeping for this church that glows on sunny afternoons and changes color throughout the day—from bright white to yellow-orange when the sun begins to set on the horizon.

Sometimes, I wish the sun would shine day and night, so I don't see the ghosts who come to haunt my evenings, like that of my Spanish grandfather, Manuel. I wish I could see the real him, not his ghost. I want him to pat me on my head, like he did when I was a child, and tell me there will be better days.

I miss the times when my grandfather and I visited El Parque Vidal in Santa Clara, thirty miles away from Remedios. That park was the center of life in that city and our special place, holding so many memories. These outings were his way to fill the void my father left when he died a few days before my eighth birthday. When we sat on a park bench under the shade of a Flamboyant tree, he would tell me stories about his beloved Spain and the life he left behind. He filled me with confidence. I could tell him anything. Since his death, I have never had that connection with anyone else.

If I had a husband with whom I could share my thoughts and fears, I suppose it might be different. But I'm single of my choosing. I must care for my mother and my elderly uncle, both devoid of happiness, except for those moments when my nieces dance in the half-empty living room. The oldest, Monica, is twelve years old and has long, black hair and intense, dark eyes that convey the maturity of a grown woman. She cares for her dreamy six-year-old sister, Andrea, who looks very different from Monica —very thin and unwilling to eat the foods we can find at the bodegas, except when her mother insists she must eat something or she will die.

I wonder what Andrea thinks when she lies down on a piece of cardboard on the sidewalk, wearing black exercise shorts and a tank top that exposes her torso. I watch her from the window to make sure she's safe out there, with her hands crossed under her head, watching the sky, and lost in thought, if I could only hear what goes through her mind during those quiet times.

"Come back inside," I say. "I don't like that outfit of yours. If you want to stay out there, you should wear something else."

"It's too hot inside."

"It's also hot outside. It's hot everywhere!"

"But here, I can watch God," she replies. "And he can see me too."

And when I hear these words, I smile. Despite the blackouts and the long lines, there is still hope for this town.

Chapter 3

La Botella (The Bottle)

(Amelia)

I open my eyes and stare at the ceiling, wondering how I'll get to work today. Will I find a way?

My cousin Lina, who lives in Havana, tells me the few buses that pass are so overcrowded that passengers spill out, clinging to doors that no longer close. Here, too, my patience and resilience are tested every day.

The house is still dark when I get out of bed, my body heavy with sleep. Dampness clings to the back of my neck and settles beneath my blue nightgown, a quiet reminder of the heat. I reach for the old alarm clock on the night table. Its white

La Botella (The Bottle)

numbers glow faintly against the black face, but the hands are hard to see. I lean closer.

Almost five.

I must hurry.

My feet slide across the floor, searching for my chancletas while one hand steadies me against the bed. I fumble for a moment before finally slipping each foot into place.

I pause and glance at my mother. She sleeps on her side, her back turned to me, her sleeveless nightgown draped loosely over her small frame. She looks so fragile now—no bigger than my twelve-year-old niece.

I tiptoe out, careful not to trip over the armless doll Andrea left on the floor. Moonlight filters through the open windows. I should have closed them. The flying roaches come in at night, bold and relentless. When they land on me, I scream as if possessed. Tonight, I see none. They must be hiding.

Waiting.

I pick up the doll so my mother won't stumble over it later, then grab her light sweater from the chair. Despite the heat, I drape it over my shoulders—armor against anything lurking in the dark.

Our Chinese kerosene lamp sits useless on the dining table. After so many blackouts, the fuel is gone.

A candle will have to do.

I light it and carry it into the kitchen. I wish I had coffee. We ran out two days ago. Yesterday's bread is all that remains.

Soon, we'll have more.

Mayda—a Cuban woman in Tampa who left over forty years ago—sent another package. It

10

La Botella (The Bottle)

should arrive next week. Coffee, beans, powdered milk. Essentials that are now luxuries. Outside the ration system, everything is too expensive. And the rations themselves are never enough: ten ounces of beans, three pounds of rice per person each month.

So there's enough for the others, I eat as little as I can.

I finish the bread quickly and head to the bathroom, candle in hand.

Fifteen minutes later, I step out into the dark streets, walking toward La Botella—the roadside stop where government vehicles and private drivers pick up passengers.

Remedios is far from Santa Clara, where I work a few days a week. The government won't hire me—not after what I wrote online about the lack of freedom.

Maybe it was foolish.

But I couldn't stay silent.

My mother says I should choose my battles.

"Mami, if we don't speak up, what will happen to my nieces? Someone has to."

"You accomplish nothing by making yourself a target," she replies.

When I arrive, several people are already waiting under the pale glow of the moon.

"Have you been waiting long?" I ask a young woman in a skirt and a white blouse.

"About fifteen minutes."

"I hope we won't have to wait much longer."

She nods.

I inhale. The scent of damp grass fills the air, sharp and clean, though it does little to soothe my allergies. I cough lightly.

11

La Botella (The Bottle)

She glances at me.

Since the pandemic, a cough in public feels like a crime.

"It's just allergies," I say.

She relaxes—but still takes a small step away.

We fall into silence.

About ten minutes later, a car pulls up beside us. The driver leans over and asks where we're going. The young woman isn't headed far. Me, on the other hand...

So it surprises me when he says, "Get in. I'll take you both."

We slide into the back seat.

It's 5:40 a.m., and the power still hasn't returned. The town lies under a black veil.

The young woman says nothing. She presses herself against the window, still wary of my cough. When she reaches her stop, the driver turns to me.

"You can sit up front," he says.

"I'm fine here," I reply. "Thank you."

He shrugs and puts the car in drive.

We leave the town behind. Moonlight washes over the shrubs and open fields. I pray for dawn to come quickly. Darkness brings out the worst in people.

Then he asks, "Are you single?"

The question makes me uneasy, though I tell myself I'm overthinking it. He watches me through the rearview mirror.

"Yes," I say.

"Family in Remedios?"

"My brother, his wife, my nieces, my mother... and an uncle."

La Botella (The Bottle)

He nods. "I'm surprised a woman like you doesn't have a husband."

"I don't have time for that," I say. "My family needs me."

He chuckles.

We turn off Avenida de los Mártires onto Circuito Norte, heading toward Highway 4-321. The questions keep coming.

"What do you do?"

"I work at a church."

"Ah." He shakes his head. "A waste of time, believing in something that doesn't exist. I believe in the Revolution. I still miss Fidel. Too bad he died."

I say nothing. If I speak, I might regret it.

"I'm a member of the Communist Party," he continues. "The Revolution has been good to Cuba."

God, give me patience.

I wonder if he waits in line for chicken, oil, or coffee. If he stands for hours under the sun only to be told there's nothing left. I wonder if he knows that feeling at all.

Then I look at his car—Russian, well-kept.

Of course.

"Listen," he says, "I'll stop in Camajuaní for coffee. Come with me."

Coffee.

I would do almost anything for a cup. But I say nothing. Instead, I lower the window and let the air hit my face. I close my eyes.

For a moment, I imagine another life—somewhere bright, somewhere free. A place like the ones I see on Facebook. Places I will never visit.

God, give me wings.

La Botella (The Bottle)

When I open my eyes, I'm still here in this car that smells faintly of burnt oil.

So I focus on what is real.

The wind against my skin. Birds are beginning to sing. The scent of wet grass, red earth, and palm trees.

Could I ever leave this and not miss it?

For a moment, I forget everything else.

"Beautiful, isn't it?" he says.

I nod.

"There's no better place on earth."

I glance at him, then roll up the window.

Camajuaní is still ahead, and I cannot afford to be late.

"You'll like the coffee," he insists.

"I don't have time."

"Come on—just a short stop. I can already smell it—the nectar of the gods. The blood of this island."

I almost shake my head. Coffee—once so common—is now a luxury.

By the time I return from work, whatever arrives at the store is gone. I wait for the weekends, when the lines are longer and the chances even smaller.

A few minutes past six, we enter Camajuaní. The town is waking up. Ahead, I spot a faded yellow school bus outside a colonial building, and people are already lined up.

"Please stop," I say. "I need to get out."

"I thought we were getting coffee."

"I can't be late. How much do I owe you?"

"Nothing. I just—"

He pulls over, but I don't let him finish.

La Botella (The Bottle)

"Thank you," I say quickly.

I step out and hurry toward the bus.

"Is this going to Santa Clara?" I ask an older woman in line.

"Yes."

"Thank God."

We board—about twenty of us. No one speaks. Some women fan themselves with pieces of cardboard.

Thirty minutes later, I arrive at the church in Santa Clara.

I split my week between here and Remedios. This one pays a little better.

Inside, the stillness washes over me like relief.

Near the altar, I follow my routine—praying for my family, for this town—then I make the sign of the cross.

Two women in their sixties kneel in silence, heads bowed, hands clasped. I pass them on my way to the office, greeting two nuns and a priest. The women smile. The priest only nods.

My office smells faintly of mold. The roof leak took too long to fix.

Still, I made it.

As I sort through the papers on my desk, my mind drifts.

I imagine a cup of coffee—hot, bitter, perfect.

Dreaming costs nothing.

But one question lingers.

How will I make it home?

La Botella (The Bottle)

Chapter 4

My Grandfather, Manuel

By Katherine Lima, translated and expanded by Betty Viamontes

(Amelia)

After everyone goes to bed, I stay in the living room alone, thinking about my grandfather. Every wall, every lamp, and the elaborate tile floors are loud reminders of him. This was the house he purchased for his family a few years before Fidel Castro came to power.

I can imagine him coming home from his bodega, tired from the long day, and sitting on his favorite chair. My mother and my uncle—who were children then—would run to him and fill him with kisses and embraces. He told me that his children erased the tiredness and gave his life meaning, as I did. Out of the many stories he shared with me, I recall one about his birthday.

***

It is February 6, 1949, and the family has started the celebration. The table is set. It's time to eat! Abuelo Manuel, his wife, their children, and some friends come and sit down. The main dish is a

17

My Grandfather, Manuel

Galician fabada, a glorious mixture of white bean soup with chorizo, blood sausage, ham, sautéed onions, garlic, salt, laurel leaves, and a pinch of saffron that infuses the senses with its exotic aromas. Accompanying the feast is white wine "Rioja," perfect for the occasion. To Abuelo Manuel, this reminds him of his Spain. Those who accompany him celebrate with joy, remembering the traditions from the homeland.

Dinner time passes between jokes and stories. To Abuelo, it seems like an eternity. Suddenly, he wants to retire but not to sleep. He doesn't know why he thinks of his land today. Lying down in bed, he remembers that day, September 7, 1923, when the ship *Infanta Isabel* left the Port of Vigo for Havana. He was only a child then and spent so many years working hard to survive.

Abuelo doesn't mind hard work, but he never cared about studying. He smiles when he evokes his mother scolding him because, again—on the way to school, he went hunting birds. He recalls his uncle Andrés' words, "Manuel, Manuel, Barcelona is good if your pockets are full."

Since the warm air of the island caressed his face for the first time, and he saw the new world, he said, "I must do what it takes to get ahead." He did it all, from working as a stevedore in the port to delivering coal, until he decided to come to Remedios.

At first, very hard years lay ahead of him. Yet a decision would mark him forever: obtaining his Naturalization Letter. He stopped being Spanish to

18

become a Cuban citizen. New rights and a future awaited. He was no longer the farmer who came from Spain to Cuba at age sixteen. He was a merchant and had a large store.

Although he respected the anthem and flag of his immigrant homeland, he loved the flag of his birthplace. He doesn't remember when he fell asleep, but he recalls crying for the land he left behind.

His family writes to him often and remembers him fondly. On the table he just imported from Spain, his black beret rests. It is one of his treasures. He tells himself, "Pontevedra, Spain, you are here forever."

The celebrations last all night. Around 6 a.m., he hears his children, Sara and Sandalio, scream, and they walk into his room to wake him.

Chapter 5

La Bodega

(Amelia)

When Castro came to power in 1959, Abuelo Manuel had already lived in Cuba for more than thirty-five years. In the 1940s, through relentless hard work, he had opened a small bodega in the town of Remedios. That bodega was his life—the realization of a dream he had carried from Spain.

La Bodega

"Manuel, I don't have the money today," Lula, a woman from our town, once told him. "Can you let me take a liter of milk? I'll pay you next week when my husband gets paid. The children need it."

Abuelo wrote her name in his ledger and handed her the milk.

Most people paid him back when they could. And even when a few didn't—like the elderly women who returned again and again with the same empty promises—he never turned them away. His generosity knew no limits. He understood what it meant to have nothing—not in his beloved Spain, and not when he arrived in the New World alone, with empty pockets and a heart full of hope.

So my grandmother was not surprised when, in 1961, the revolutionaries came to take his bodega.

"The revolution now owns this business," one of them said. "You may continue working here as an employee. Everyone must support the people's revolution."

Abuelo adjusted his glasses and placed the keys in the official's hand.

"If this will help the people of Remedios," he said quietly, "I will do what I must."

From that day on, he earned only a fraction of what he once made as the rightful owner.

A few years later, after thousands had fled the island, he considered returning to Spain. But leaving would have meant admitting failure. He had become a Cuban citizen. Why not stay and try to make a life here?

By the time he understood what he had lost, it was too late.

His roots were now in Cuba. His children were grown, with families of their own. They were Cuban by birth and by heart. Even if he had wanted to leave, he no longer had the means.

So, he remained in Remedios, standing behind the counter of a bodega that was no longer his, staring at shelves that grew emptier with each passing year.

Abuelo died in 1998, during the Special Period, when the fall of the Soviet Union cut off the subsidies that had sustained Cuba.

Mamá says it was a heart attack.

I believe it was hunger.

The entire town came to his funeral.

That night, after we returned home, there was a knock at the door. My mother opened it.

It was Lula—now in her sixties.

"I came to repay what I owe Manuel," she said. "He let me take food on credit almost forty years ago, and I never paid him. Even though he is gone, I want to settle my debt with his family. Your father was an angel."

A tear rolled down my mother's cheek as she took the money.

"Please," she said softly, "come in. Let me make you some coffee."

Chapter 6

Bath at Midnight

(Amelia)

At midnight, Andrea—my six-year-old niece—wakes me.

"Tía Amelia, can you shine a light on me while I bathe?"

After a day without electricity, she wants to use the little "trick" I taught her—to bathe and lie down wet, hoping to ease the heat and keep the mosquitoes away.

I light a candle and ask her to be quiet, so she doesn't wake the rest of the house. Then I lead her to the bathroom.

She undresses and begins pouring cold water over her small body with a can. She is so thin I can see every rib.

"Do you need help, my love?" I ask gently.

"No, Auntie. I can do it myself."

When she finishes, I walk her back to her room. Still wet, she lies down on her thin mattress.

I lean over to kiss her goodnight.

"Auntie," she whispers, "will this ever end?"

My heart tightens.

"You must pray, my love," I tell her softly. "You must pray."

Bath at Midnight

For years, it was only the adults who asked how long we would endure the blackouts, the endless lines, the hunger.

Now, even the children are asking.

And no matter who comes to me, my answer remains the same:

You must pray.

From my small town of Remedios, I lift my voice to God—for our nation, for children like my nieces, already weary of hunger, already tired of living in the dark.

Chapter 7

Explosions

(Amelia)

Black clouds over Havana after explosions

Staying hopeful, for those of us in Remedios—and across this island—is as essential as
breathing. We must believe that life will improve,
that the blackouts are temporary. We hold on to the

idea that food will one day be affordable, that water will flow when we need it most.

And then, just when I thought things could not get worse, the news came.

The unthinkable had happened.

At first, I didn't believe it would affect us here in Remedios. We are far—185 kilometers—from where it began. But soon, black clouds appeared, spreading across the island.

They called it a freak accident.

On the afternoon of August 5, 2022, lightning struck a crude oil tank at a supertanker terminal in the industrial zone of Matanzas. Strong winds pushed the flames toward nearby fuel reserves, triggering a series of explosions. By the next morning, dozens were injured, some critically. Seventeen firefighters were missing.

We watched in horror.

A massive fireball threatened the island's fragile electrical system. At first, I believed it would be contained quickly. But when all efforts failed, the government was forced to seek international assistance.

Soon, a dense cloud of black smoke drifted toward Havana, home to millions. Reports warned of toxic chemicals in the air. I couldn't stop wondering what this would mean—not just now, but years from now.

As the fires raged, other countries sent aid—industrial foam, equipment, experts—anything to help bring the flames under control.

By August 9, more than a hundred people had been injured, and lives had been lost. After five days, the worst fire in Cuba's history was finally contained. But the damage was immense. Nearly forty percent of the island's main fuel storage had been destroyed.

The blackouts that followed were relentless—especially in towns like Remedios.

Slowly, the black clouds faded to gray, then disappeared. Sunlight returned.

But the damage remained.

I found myself wondering how long it would take to rebuild—how long before life, if not normal, at least bearable, could return.

Still, I must look ahead.

When summer ends, cooler days will come. The nights will be easier. We will breathe a little more freely.

And I will continue to pray—for this town, for my family, for this island and its people—that we may endure, and that we may never lose hope.

Chapter 8

The Last Two Buns

(Amelia)

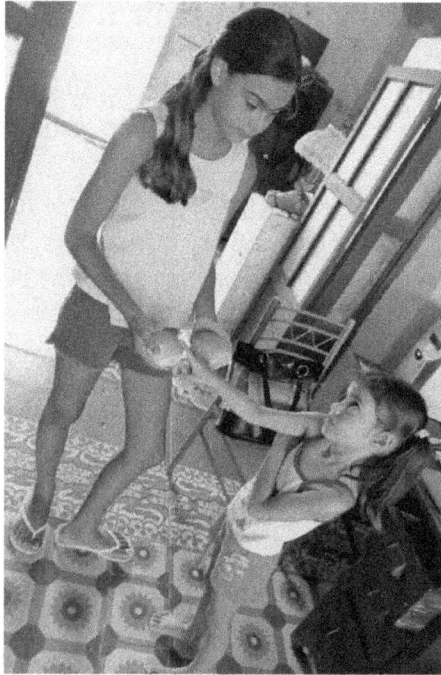

I watch Mónica and Andrea dancing in the living room. Andrea is barefoot, her brown ponytail bouncing as she spins. Mónica tries to teach her a new set of moves, but Andrea refuses to follow.

"No, that's not how you do it," Mónica says. "Watch me and try again."

She demonstrates the short routine once more.

"Your turn."

"I won't. I'll do it my way."

Mónica insists for a little while longer, but Andrea ignores her, moving wildly, out of rhythm—as if she had eaten a pound of sugar.

After a few minutes, Andrea slows down, breathless. She turns to her sister.

"I'm hungry."

Mónica looks at me.

I shake my head and sigh. Then I remember. "I brought some bread from the store, but it didn't look very good."

Mónica disappears into the kitchen and returns with two buns. She studies them carefully. One is clearly better than the other.

She holds them out to Andrea.

"Which one do you want?"

Andrea looks at both, hesitates—and then, with quiet guilt, chooses the one that isn't moldy.

Chapter 9

No Parranda in 2022?

In October, the news spread quickly through town: the Parranda—Remedios' beloved, carnival-like celebration—had been canceled due to financial constraints.

The reaction was immediate. People took to social media to express their outrage and disappointment.

Since 2018, UNESCO has recognized the Parrandas of Remedios as part of the Intangible Cultural Heritage of Humanity. Now, just two months before the festivities, many asked the same question:

How could something so important—so celebrated around the world—be allowed to disappear for lack of government funding?

A Facebook post lamenting the cancellation went viral. Criticism grew louder, spreading beyond the town and reaching the highest levels of government.

For more than two centuries, the Parrandas—with their elaborate pyrotechnics, traditions, and rivalries—had defined the identity of Remedios. Entire neighborhoods, divided into two competing groups, spent months preparing for the event:

building floats, designing banners, crafting lan-
terns, rehearsing music and dance.

Now, everything was on hold.

The frustration only intensified.

Eventually, the government responded and
secured funding to revive the celebration.

But not everyone welcomed the decision.

Some residents saw the Parranda not as a
source of pride, but as a source of disorder—noise,
chaos, and an overwhelming police presence. Men
in olive-green uniforms would surround the square,
watching, listening, monitoring.

"I understand why they funded it," an old man
said, speaking to a friend in the park.

"It's part of who we are," the other replied. "It
makes us proud."

"Not anymore," the first man said. "It's a dis-
traction. Something to keep people occupied. What
we need is food—not parties."

"I know," his friend answered. "But I'm tired
of waiting for a miracle. At least for a few nights, we
can dance. We can forget. And maybe—when these
children grow up—they'll bring the change we've
been waiting for."

"Keep dreaming, my friend."

The two men fell silent.

Nearby, a young couple stopped in front of a
colonial house and kissed under the fading light.

Chapter 10

The Note

(Amelia)

After waiting in a long line to buy my ration of groceries, I walk to Martí Park, my bags heavy in my hands, my feet aching. I look for a place to rest.

A family of five passes by on their way to the pavilion, laughing softly, but I choose a spot along the salmon-colored wall that surrounds a giant oak tree. The shade offers relief from the harsh afternoon sun.

As I sit, catching my breath, I scan my surroundings.

That's when I notice it—a folded piece of paper on a nearby bench.

It stirs my curiosity.

Perhaps a student left it. Or an elderly person. I lean forward, pick it up, and unfold it.

The words are written carefully, in black ink. I begin to read.

We lost the ball game—just as we have lost our dignity.

Every morning, we lose our breath trying to get to work early, only to find that our wages cannot keep up with the cost of living.

We watch the happiness fade from our children's faces when they cannot have candy or a piece of cake on their birthdays.

Our own happiness disappears in long lines, in arguments, in the struggle to buy a small quota of food—barely enough for a family of three.

Every afternoon, we lose a piece of our soul trying to get home—waiting for buses that may never come, searching for medicine that cannot be found.

At night, we lose hope as we put our children to bed in the heat without electricity.

We cannot move forward.

The only option left is to leave—to go to that place our rulers call "hell." But in that "hell," my son will eat the sweets he asks for every night. He will live in freedom. He will have a future.

I invite you to live in Cuba. Let us trade places. I believe my son would be happier where you are.

—Chester

I fold the paper carefully and place it in my purse.

Then I wipe away a tear.

Chapter 11

The Cat

(Amelia)

I am about to open the front door after returning from the bodega when we hear it—a faint cry.

Mónica takes the groceries inside, then follows Andrea and me across the street, searching for the sound.

For a moment, it disappears.

We stop and look around.

The Cat

Then we hear it again.

"It's coming from over there!" Andrea says, running toward it.

"Be careful!" I call after her.

We find it in an empty lot across from the house, hidden beneath a pile of trash. Gently, I push the debris aside with my foot, careful not to hurt it.

At last, I see him—a small, trembling creature with soft fur and kind, frightened eyes.

"What's wrong, little one?" I whisper. "Who left you here?"

He tries to stand, but his legs give out beneath him. A weak, painful cry escapes him—one that seems to echo through my chest.

"He's hurt," I say. "Someone must have kicked him."

The girls kneel beside him, stroking his tiny head. He doesn't resist.

"Can we take him home?" Andrea asks. "Please, Tía Amelia."

I already know the answer.

Too many animals are abandoned here—left behind by people who can barely feed themselves. But the way he looks at us, the quiet trust in his eyes, makes it impossible to walk away.

"Yes," I say softly. "Let's take him home."

I bring a clean rag from the house and wrap him gently in it. His body is so light—too light. Every bone beneath his fur tells the same story.

When we walk inside, my mother and uncle smile at the sight of him.

"Can I play with him?" Andrea asks.

"Let me bathe him first," I say.

"And trim his claws," my mother adds. "He might get scared."

"I will. I don't want him to hurt the girls."

I bathe him carefully while the girls prepare a small plate of leftover food and water. I give him a bit of medicine for the pain.

By the next morning, he has a name—Misu—and there is already a spark of life in him. He tries to stand again. This time, his legs hold him for a few seconds.

"A few more days," Mónica says, smiling, "and he'll be like new."

The girls make him a bed from old rags inside a broken plastic container. It isn't much, but Misu curls into it as if it were the softest place in the world.

A week later, he jumps onto my mother's lap. She strokes his fur, and he leans into her touch, purring softly.

She looks at me and nods.

"It's the best gift you could have given me," she says. "We may not have much food, but here, he will never lack love. That no one can take away from us."

I nod.

Because I know that the day we lose our compassion—our humanity—there will be nothing left.

Chapter 12

Matilda's Granddaughter

Matilda watches her granddaughter dance in the living room. Although Clarita is only twelve, she is already blossoming into a beautiful young woman. The tall, thin girl with almond-shaped café con leche eyes moves rhythmically to the music. Her smile beams and fills the room.

Matilda wishes the girl had not left childish things behind so quickly. She senses that womanhood will inject the fibers of her innocence with the harsh reality of life. But Matilda fears it is too late. The only rag doll the girl owns now collects dust in a corner of the bedroom.

"You remind me so much of your mother," Maltilda says as she irons a blouse."

"That's what you always say, Abuela. And I want to be a great dancer like her." Clarita smiles and continues to sway to the music on the radio.

"I don't like you dancing like that. You are too young. And those shorts are too tight. Go change into something else."

"Everyone my age dresses like me. It's not a big deal. I don't want to look like an old woman."

"At your age, I wore beautiful dresses cinched at the waist. Young ladies behaved properly and didn't wear clothes that revealed too much. I miss those times."

37

Matilda's Granddaughter

Clarita doesn't miss a step as she dances to the music, yet she still replies.

"Many years have passed, Abuela. Now women can be soldiers, doctors, and scientists."

Matilda sighs as she observes Clarita's long, black hair, which now reaches to the middle of her back. It remains shiny and healthy despite the lack of shampoo.

"I don't know what I'm going to do with you. I'm always so worried."

"No need to be worried. I study, get good grades, and go to church with you when you ask me, but I also like to have a little fun. What's wrong with that?"

Matilda watches her dance and thinks of Clarita's mother. She indeed favors her. It's like watching her when she was that age; she was indeed a skillful dancer. They remain in silence until the song ends, and Clarita walks over to her grandmother and kisses her on the cheek.

"You are the best grandmother in the world. You know that?"

"And you, the best granddaughter. I want to protect you. That's all."

"I am only trying to get ready for the Parranda. My friends and I are rehearsing for it. I can't wait!"

"Are you planning to dance like that in public? I can understand you dancing here, in the privacy of your home, but not in front of strange men. It's not lady-like."

Clarita squeezes her grandmother's wrinkled face.

"That's why I love you so much! You are so protective."

Matilda's Granddaughter

The girl stands very close to Matilda, who glances at her and caresses her face.

"Don't you miss her?" Matilda asks.

"Who?"

"Your *real* grandmother? She adored you, you know."

"I was seven. And yes, I miss her, but you have been here for as long as I can remember. I am so lucky to have you."

"I am not your real grandmother, my love. She was."

"She never loved me as you do."

"She wasn't capable, not after it all happened. You are too young to understand. When you are older and more mature, it will all become clear. I hope you never lose everything dear to you."

"All I know is that I never want to lose you. That's what matters."

Clarita embraces her grandmother, while Matilda inhales, wondering what will happen to her granddaughter once she is gone. God knows she does not have much longer. Who will care for Clarita, then?

Chapter 13

The Visitor

(Amelia)

I am returning from the bodega empty-handed after a failed attempt to purchase tomato sauce. Frustrated, I notice the groups of people gathered around the square to watch the preparations for the Parranda, trucks full of fireworks and workers assembling the intricate displays—taller than the churches—which, on December 24th, will illuminate the town. Excitement floods the center of the city of Remedios.

Next to José Martí Park, across from colonial buildings, stands a unique replica of Lady Liberty, made by the Italian sculptor Carlos Nicoly Manfredy. It has been standing on this square since 1906. Instead of a symbol of freedom, the government called it the Monument to the Martyrs of San Juan de los Remedios. Unlike on other days, when I marveled at the beauty and resilience of this statue, I pass by without looking at it, thinking about the pot of black beans I left soaking in water and the key ingredient I lack to cook them properly.

As I try to avoid the people standing on the square, I think about the history of these celebrations and the unintended consequences of a priest's actions.

40

The Visitor

This festival started over 200 years ago, in 1820, when a young priest, Padre Francisco Vigil de Quiñones, hoping to attract parishioners during the low-attendance period of December 16 until Christmas, asked the children to go out in the streets and make noise with cans full of rocks, horns, and any noisemaker they could find. Over the years, organized music bands replaced the noisy children, and the idea spread beyond Remedios and throughout the island.

In 1851, two rival groups representing the neighborhoods of El Carmen and San Salvador formed, each with its own performers and floats, competing to provide the best entertainment and displaying their flags. A globe and a brown flag represent El Carmen. A rooster and a red flag symbolize San Salvador. In 1921, for the first time, flashing lights lit up the monumental displays. Unlike the floats of a typical carnival, the floats of the Parranda always represent a story, mythological, historical, or current.

To this day, by the end of the yearly celebration, each group proclaims itself the winner.

However, the economic situation over the past 60 years has affected this traditional celebration, limiting its scope. I wish they would disappear altogether. I don't care for the festivities. For several days, the town is turned upside down. Then, on the 24th of December, the town fills with music, noise, dancing, and drinking late into the night, upsetting many long-term residents and me.

As I think about the unintended consequences of the priest's actions, one of the people in the square runs into me.

41

The Visitor

"Excuse me," he says. "I was so busy watching the displays that I didn't see where I was going. My sincere apologies."

The gentleman, in his sixties, smells of cologne and dresses better than others in town, with a guayabera shirt and dark grey pants with perfect creases.

"Don't worry. Enjoy the festivities," I say.

As I begin to walk away, I hear his voice.

"Miss, could you help me?"

I turn around and glance at him as if to ascertain his intentions.

"I am not here for the celebrations. I came to visit the place where my mother was born. I live in Miami now."

"Oh, you are here from the United States?"

A nervous smile replaces my frustration, and for a moment, I forget about the tomato sauce.

"I am. I was born in Havana. I left as a child, alone, during the Pedro Pan exodus. My parents stayed here."

"Did they eventually leave?" I ask with honest curiosity.

"It's a long story, but no. I am here trying to reconstruct the pieces. My mother was born in Remedios. I wanted to see what her eyes saw when she lived here."

"Is she dead?"

"Yes."

"I'm so sorry." I nervously consult my watch.

"Are you in a hurry?" he says.

"I am returning from the store. I wanted to buy tomato sauce for the lunch I'm preparing for my family, but they don't have any."

"I'm sorry. I wish I could help you. Actually, I went to a store in Santa Clara yesterday that might have it."

"That's too far. And it's probably very expensive. Don't worry. We are used to inventing. Do you need some help?"

"I want to ask the people in town if they knew my mother. After everything happened, she left Havana and returned here."

"What was her name?"

"Alicia Rodríguez Campos."

"That name is familiar." I hesitate for a moment. "Look, I'm embarrassed to take you to my house. It is very modest. However, my mother and uncle might have known her."

"You don't need to be embarrassed, but I would hate to impose."

"Don't worry. We don't live far from here. Please come with me."

We walk for a few minutes, leaving the square and the noise behind, and turn into a narrow street lined with colonial-style row houses. Some have fresh paint, but most are unpainted, with mold and mildew stains.

"It's quiet on this street," he observes.

"Not for long. When the music starts, we won't be able to sleep."

"This is a very popular town. I hear that it is a world heritage site," he says.

"Some heritage," I reply, rolling my eyes.

I stop in front of one of the houses and insert a key in the keyhole. When I was growing up, my mother never locked the door, but with deepening shortages, assaults, and robberies have become more common. Although I heard crime was much worse in Havana.

"Mami, Tio, I'm home, and we have a visitor," I announce, and pointing to a rocking chair in the small living room, I add, "Please have a seat. I would bring some coffee, but we ran out. However, I could offer you a glass of water, and if my nieces didn't eat them, we might have a couple of cookies that a woman I met on Facebook sent us."

"I'm not here to take your food. Don't worry. I'm fine."

My mother and my uncle appear moments later, each aided by a walker, both pale and thin, with sunken eyes. I pull a couple of chairs for them and help them sit down.

The visitor stands and shakes my mother's and my uncle's hands, who glance at him shyly, as if realizing he is not from Remedios.

"My name is Frank. I just realized that I didn't ask the young woman for her name. Where are my manners?"

"My name is Sara. This is my brother Sandalio, and that young woman is my daughter. Her name is Amelia."

"Well, Mami, I'm not so young anymore," I respond. "Mami, where are my nieces and their parents?"

"They all went out to watch the preparations. You know the girls. They are restless, especially the youngest."

Frank looks at the pictures on the unpainted walls as if trying to discover a familiar face.

"Thank you for inviting me to your house, Amelia. I don't want to take up too much of your time. Ms. Sara, I wanted to know if you knew Alicia Rodriguez Campos. She died about five years ago."

"The name is familiar," my mother says. "Do you have a picture?"

Frank retrieves his wallet from his pocket and takes out a small picture. He hands it to her, and she examines it.

"I remember her," she says. "Her husband was jailed and killed in front of the firing squad."

Frank looks down.

"Yes, he was. When I was in my twenties and thirties, I traveled to Havana several times and looked for her. No one knew where she had gone. I don't like social media much, but I recently joined a group and started asking people about her. Someone finally said she had come here."

"She did," my mother replies. "She talked about you a lot. After sending you alone to the United States, she tried to find you through the church. They said you had been placed with a family but ran away."

"That's right. I moved in with one of my teachers. I didn't know how to find her. During my last trip to Havana, I learned that she had died here. Do you know where she lived? Did she remarry?"

"If I remember correctly, she lived with a second or third cousin close to here, Matilda, I think. I don't think that your mom remarried."

"Was she related to Matilda?" I ask. "I know, Matilda! She comes to church with her granddaughter."

"Could you show me where she lives and maybe introduce me to her?" Frank asks me.

"I have to cook for the family," I explain. "Maybe later."

"No! You go with the gentleman right now," my mother replies. "You are too young to stay in this house cooking and cleaning like a maid. Then, you work all week. How long? She is not even married!"

"Mami, please!"

"Let's do this," Frank says. "It's still early. If you like, I could come back in a couple of hours, so you have time to make dinner. I don't want to impact your routine. Would you mind if I took you to lunch before we visit Matilda? In the meantime, I will try to find the tomato sauce and coffee."

"I appreciate that, but I cannot allow you to do that," I say.

"Don't cook and go with the gentleman," my mother repeats. "God knows you are not getting any younger. You should also go to the Parranda with him on the 24th instead of staying in your room with sheets over your head. Live a little!"

"Amelia," my uncle says. "You know how much I love you, but you're not going to win this one. Just go out. When was the last time you went out to eat?"

"And maybe you can tell me about the legends of this town," Frank suggests. "I heard about a couple of them, but I would like to hear your version. It would mean a lot to me."

"Are you married?" my mother asks Frank.

"Mami, are you serious?" I say, crossing my arms.

"I don't mind answering the question. My wife passed away three years ago. A car accident."

"I'm so sorry," I say.

46

The Visitor

"I am, too," Frank replies. "She was the love of my life."

"Frank," I say, "if you like, I can accompany you to Matilda's house, but I will not take advantage of your generosity."

"I insist."

I nod. "Fine then. You can return in a couple of hours," I say. "And Mami, you and I need to talk."

Frank leaves the house moments later. I then argue with my mother about what I call her "inappropriate behavior" until my uncle interrupts them and announces, "I'm going to my room to listen to the radio."

***

By the time Frank returned, my brother, Hector, and his family had arrived. My sister-in-law is in the kitchen getting ready to serve the lunch I prepared. Hector practices dance choreography with his daughters, while my mother and my uncle, sitting across from them, smile and clap as they watch. The twelve-year-old and her father dance in synchronized fashion, but the six-year-old makes a series of clownish movements, mocking the other two and trying to get their attention.

My sister-in-law opens the door and announces the visitor's arrival. When the girls notice Frank, the music stops. My mother introduces Frank to everyone, and the greetings begin.

Frank hands Hector a bag of groceries.

"Amelia needed tomato sauce and coffee, but I bought a few more things like red beans, rice, pork, and chicken."

The Visitor

"That's too much, Frank," my mother says. "You shouldn't have."

"It's no trouble at all."

My brother thanks Frank and excuses himself for a moment to take the groceries to the kitchen. He returns moments later.

"Well, now that we have coffee, can I offer you some?" my mother asks.

"No, thank you. As much as I enjoy having two or three cups a day, I'm going to reserve the next one for after lunch."

The family and Frank all sit wherever they can find a chair. The girls sit on the tiled floor across from Frank, watching him with curiosity. My mother asks Frank questions about Miami and Frank's life and marvels at his stories.

"Do you need a ration card to buy groceries in Miami?" the oldest girl asks.

"Of course not," her father replies. "Only here, Monica."

"Is the milk available to everyone, or is it restricted to children and the elderly?" Monica asks.

"It's available to everyone," Frank replies.

"Wow! If I lived in a place with so much milk, I would drink three tall glasses a day!" Andrea, the youngest girl, says, speaking with her hands.

A short silence follows. Moments later, I make my entrance into the living room. All heads turn to me.

"Tía Amelia!" Andrea says. "You look so beautiful. You never wear makeup. And you let your hair down! It looks so pretty. Where are you going? Are we going with you?"

I smile shyly. "No, you are staying here."

"Are you going on a date?" Monica whispers.

"No more questions!" I reply.

With my purse strap looping over my shoulder, I hurriedly kiss my family goodbye and depart with Frank.

"Have fun!" my mother says before I wave to my family and close the door.

Chapter 14

The Restaurant

(Amelia)

We arrive at the Ebenezer Restaurant located at the Finca (Farm) Villa Felipa in Remedios by car. Frank's driver, an elderly gentleman from town whom Frank contracted to drive him around, leaves us in front. On either side of the covered entrance, which rises above the roofline and forms a triangular top, we see the old red-tiled roof. It is evident that the house's owner built a wraparound porch with a wooden veranda to accommodate the restaurant and surrounded it with colorful foliage.

When we enter, a young waiter dressed in black pants, a black vest, and a white shirt greets us with a friendly smile and leads us to our table, one of several varnished black tables surrounded by matching chairs.

"Have you been here before?" I ask Frank.

"No, but I read about it in a tourist guide."

I feel uncomfortable. I have not been to a restaurant in over twenty years—such a waste of money when one could cook at home. Then, I wonder, *with what?* And I think about the tomato sauce I could not find that morning.

"I heard you say that you were able to find the tomato sauce and brought us other groceries. How much do I owe you?"

"It's a gift."

"But why?"

"You have been very nice and helpful since we met, so I simply wanted to show you my gratitude. I am glad to find a friend in the place my mother called home once."

"That's very kind of you. Thank you."

He opens the menu the waiter left us, but I don't open mine.

"Aren't you going to order something?" he asks.

"I'll order the same as you. I'm not picky."

"Are you sure? There are some nice selections."

"I'm sure. Thank you."

Moments later, the white-haired owner of the family-owned restaurant comes over and greets us with a smile. He asks us where we are from, and when he learns that Frank is from the United States, his eyes light up. It's as if a good friend has come to see him. He firmly shakes Frank's hand and enthusiastically asks him about life abroad and his profession.

"I'm a retired CPA," he says.

"CPA?"

"Accountant. Well, I managed the accounting department at a hospital. And yes, life has been good. It would have been better if I had my parents with me, but they are both dead."

"I'm sorry about your parents. I just wanted to welcome you personally to my humble restaurant. Do you have any questions about the menu? Or better yet, what would I recommend?"

"Sure," Frank says.

"The pork steak with fried plantains, rice, and beans is delicious," the owner replies.

Frank looks at me, seeking my approval. I nod.

"In that case, we will both have what you are recommending."

After the owner walks away, Frank doesn't waste much time. "Now, tell me about some of the legends of this town."

"There are so many. One of them is about the Iglesia de la Virgen del Buen Viaje. I'm sure you noticed that Remedios has two churches in the same square. In fact, it is the only town in Cuba where this is the case."

"So why two churches?"

"The legend is that back in the 1800s, offshore fishermen who were traveling in a fragile vessel were caught in a storm. As they prepared to return to the sea, they spotted a large wooden trunk drifting among the waves. Inside it, they found a beautiful image of the Virgin Mary carved in wood. They credited the Virgin with their good fortune. Despite traveling in a fragile vessel, they had reached shore safely. The fishermen arrived in Remedios via a river that no longer exists and decided to give the virgin to a black man who lived near it. A priest told the black man that the statue belonged to the church and took it from him. The next day, the priest noticed that the statue was gone. He returned to the black man's house and found it there. The people in town thought that the Virgin herself had chosen where she wanted to stay, so a second church was built in the same square."

He then asks me about Remedio's ghosts and the tunnels that run beneath the town. Thoughts of my grandfather rush to my mind. That's all that's left of him. Soon, that's all that will be left of all of us.

The waiter, bringing two plates full of steaming food, interrupts our conversation. The pork steak on my plate is enough to feed my family of seven.

"So much food," I say, inhaling the glorious odor of sauteed onions, garlic, and spices I don't recognize. He smiles.

After I eat the first bite, my eyes fill with tears as I think about my nieces, but I don't want to appear ungrateful and take the second bite. I eat slowly, savoring every bite.

Frank thanks me again for helping him.

"It is you who helped us. You're like an angel that God placed in our path."

"Are you religious?"

"Yes, I practically live in the church, especially during the preparations for special events like Good Friday or Christmas. It isn't easy to get teenagers to do what we want. They have their agenda and listen to no one."

"I know what you mean, and I don't miss those times. I'm glad my children are grown and have their own families. Now they can experience what their mother and I did when they were growing up."

After eating half of the food on my plate, I stop.

The Restaurant

"You don't like it?" he asks.

"Oh, yes, I do. Very much. But after eating so little every day, I think my stomach must have shrunk. I will take the rest home. I'll put the leftovers in the refrigerator when we get to Matilda's house."

When he has consumed all the food on his plate, he asks, "Do you want a flan?"

My eyes open wide. I haven't had a flan for years. He smiles.

"No need to answer. Your expression says it all. I'll order two flans."

I feel embarrassed. My mother always tells me that my face is an open book.

"This is going to cost a fortune," I said.

"It's not very expensive. Don't worry."

"For those of us who live here, it is. To give you an idea, I earn 2,500 pesos a month. When oil doesn't come to the stores, I must pay around 1,200 pesos for a liter of soy oil."

"Soy oil?"

"That's what's available."

"I use olive oil. It's good for your health."

"We don't have choices here. Many times, my nieces eat only rice and fried plantains for dinner. No protein. Eggs and meat are luxuries."

"I didn't know things had gotten this bad, and I'm truly sorry."

"I'm the one who should be sorry for telling you about our problems. We should talk about vampires and ghosts. This town is full of stories."

I then share with him the legend of the "Screamer of Seborucal."

54

The Restaurant

During the 17th century, pirates would arrive in Remedios to rob and attack its inhabitants. One of the most notable pirates, Francisco Náu, aided by his men, captured, raped, enslaved women, and destroyed everything in his path.

In the town of Seborucal lived a beautiful young woman with long black hair, pale skin, and large black eyes. Francisco fell in love with her and tried to force himself on her. She scratched his face and ran. Francisco was furious and ordered his men to follow her and kill her. According to the legend, Francisco's men decapitated the young woman. While holding her severed head in her hands, she kept screaming until her body collapsed. People rumored that from that day on, after midnight, her screams could be heard. Everyone believes that the ghost of the screamer of Seborucal still roams the town.

"What an interesting and implausible story."

"I have done some research on the matter. Dutch researchers studying rats found evidence that the rats' brains continue to generate some electrical activity for a few seconds after the head is separated from the body."

Frank giggles.

"This conversation really took a wrong turn. From misery to decapitation."

I cover my mouth to conceal my giggle, and my face reddens.

"I need to go out more often. I have completely failed," I say.

"It's not so bad. Unusual subject to discuss over lunch, but interesting nonetheless."

I can no longer conceal my amusement and start laughing, and he laughs with me. I cannot remember the last time I laughed so much, and it feels good. That feeling is enhanced when the flans arrive, and I take a bite.

I have read that our mood makes food taste different and that people who suffer from depression have lower-than-usual levels of serotonin in the brain. Although undiagnosed, I have always believed that I suffer from depression, but on this day, my taste buds seem unaffected. They fully experience the heavenly taste of the sweet mixture of condensed and evaporated milk, eggs, vanilla, and sugar. I close my eyes for a moment and smile.

"Extraordinary," I say.

"I'm so glad you like it."

I thank him again. To conclude the meal, he orders coffee for both of us. But this is not the coffee we have at home. The smoky, burnt aroma, along with the dark roast's sweet taste, stimulates all my senses.

At the conclusion of our meal, I asked the waiter for a container to take half of my food home. By then, the driver will be outside, waiting to take us to our next destination.

Chapter 15

The Line

Rogelio leaves the house before dawn. His steps are tired, and his body moves unevenly, aided by a wooden cane he made himself. His stomach growls when he smells the aroma of coffee that emanates from one of the houses along the way. He then hears a familiar voice behind him.

"Rogelio, where are you going this early?"

He stops and looks around. Everything is still dark, but he recognizes the silhouette of Prematuro. Prematuro has become a permanent fixture in the town of Remedios, an adoptive son, mysterious and obnoxious, trapped in his own world. His real name is Alejandro López, but people call him El Prema or Prematuro. The reasons are unclear. He is foul-mouthed when poked and boasts an enormous tongue due to his macroglossia disorder, a tongue he doesn't mind showing to the people in town.

Prematuro came to Remedios in search of a job during the Special Period. He must have been in his early twenties then, black-skinned, muscular, and wide-eyed.

Rogelio and his wife pitied him and occasionally gave him a plate of soup, watching him eat it with desperation.

"I'm going to buy my monthly quota of groceries," Rogelio says.

"Get ready to wait a while."

Rogelio nods and shows him the white sack he carries.

"I brought some water with me," Rogelio says. "Are you working today?"

"No. I have nothing to do today, but I'd be happy to keep you company if you'd like. I enjoy listening to all the gossip in town. It makes time go by faster."

"God knows that's all that's left in this town: gossip."

"And if this economic situation continues, even gossip will be leaving this town and going to the United States."

"Do you want to go there?"

"Are you kidding? Who doesn't?"

"I'm too old to go anywhere," Rogelio replies.

Rogelio resumes his walk.

"Are you going to the Parranda this year?" Prematuro asks.

"I'm too old for parties. Eighty-one springs already. All that music, dancing, and fireworks... all that makes me nervous. I'm not the man I used to be. That's for sure. Are you going?"

"And you think I'm going to miss the opportunity to show the ladies my moves? I'm a great dancer. The best dancer in the world!"

"In the world? I guess you don't need a grandmother," Rogelio replies.

Prematuro looks at him in confusion, as if he has failed to understand this commonly used phrase. Grandmothers are always complimentary to their grandchildren.

"Of course I do. Everybody needs one, but she's gone. I only have my mom left. She lives in Santa Clara, and she is sick. I keep asking the priest to do a special mass for her. God will hear him and cure her. I don't think he's listening to me."

Rogelio stops for a moment and pats Prematuro on his back. "You're a good man. Don't you let anyone tell you otherwise."

"I don't think the people in this town like me much. Some of them laugh at me, you know. They don't think I'm too smart. I've heard them."

"Don't let them get to you. They don't know you as I do."

When the men arrive at the bodega, there are about thirty people in line.

"I hope they have chicken today," Rogelio says.

"You know what I really feel like eating?"

"What?"

"A steak. I only had it once in my life."

"When was that?"

"I was living in Santa Clara. I was about ten and carried the bags for a tourist and his family. We started talking, and he invited me to lunch. I still remember that juicy steak with lots of onions and fried potatoes."

"Prematuro," a middle-aged woman with plump cheeks who waits in front of Prematuro and Rogelio says, "out of all the people in town, the last person I thought would have enjoyed a piece of steak was you. Are you sure you are not making that up?"

"Teresa," Rogelio says, "why would you say that? Have you ever had a steak?"

"It's been years since the last time, but I have."

"Well, good for you. Stop bothering the young man."

"Why would you care?" Teresa says. "It's none of your business."

"He's my friend, and I love him like a son. That's why."

She waves her hand in dismissal and turns around.

"Do you really feel that way about me?" Prematuro asks Rogelio.

"I do."

Prematuro smiles like a child and takes a couple of nervous steps. As dawn approaches, the line gets longer. By the time the bodega opens at eight, Rogelio turns around and can no longer see where the line ends.

"Do you have your ration card?" Rogelio asks Prematuro.

"I do, but I don't have enough money."

"I don't have enough myself, but if I can spare some, I will lend it to you. If you wait for another day, there may not be any food left."

Prematuro agrees.

After a while, the line begins to move. The excitement is palpable.

"I hope they have chicken today," Rogelio repeats.

The line moves slowly, and soon the sun begins to shine on the people in line. People block it from their eyes with their hands.

At last, Rogelio's turn arrives.

"I need your ration card," the attendant, a thin, bald guy in his late forties, says.

Rogelio hands it to him. The attendant examines it and consults a list. Then, he returns the card to Rogelio without marking anything.

"I can't give you the groceries today," he says. "The records show that you are deceased."

"Dead?" Rogelio replies. "Do I look dead to you? I may be old, but not dead."

"Sorry, compañero (comrade). The list says you are dead." Raising his chin, he glances at the person behind Rogelio. "Next person."

"Rogelio is my friend," Prematuro says. "He's alive. You see? He is talking. He's walking. He can dance too, you know?"

"Prematuro, I'm not going to argue with you," the attendant replies. "Are you buying anything today?"

Rogelio shakes his head and takes some money out of his pockets.

"Here. Buy your groceries for the month. Otherwise, they may run out."

"What about you?"

"I must go to the authorities and explain what happened. There isn't much more I can do."

Prematuro buys his quota, including some chicken.

After they leave the bodega, Prematuro says, "I promise I'll pay you back. Sometimes, I do work for tourists, and they pay me. I also know how to do repairs. You see my muscles?"

"I know. You are very strong. That's good. I was strong too when I was your age, but the years don't forgive."

Prematuro shrugs. "I won't keep the chicken," Prematuro says. "I'll let you keep it."

"That's your quota."

"I can get a female tourist to take me to lunch. There are some lonely women out there. They like my muscles and how I dance. Sometimes, they take me to their room at their hotel."

"To their hotel room?" Rogelio's eyes open wide. "You must be careful. You're going to get one of those diseases."

"I'll be fine. I'm strong as an ox."

Prematuro accompanies Rogelio back home and gives him the chicken. A few days later, he returns with the money he owes Rogelio.

"Did you straighten everything out?" Prematuro asks him.

"It took me a few days, but this morning, they gave me a paper to show that I'm indeed alive. I'll go to the store this afternoon."

Prematuro volunteers to go with him. The line is longer than before, and when Rogelio's turn to buy his groceries arrives, he learns there is almost nothing left. The chicken is gone.

He returns home with a few pounds of rice and some sugar.

"I'll see if one of my tourist friends can get you what you are missing," Prematuro says.

"Don't worry, son. There is always next month."

Rogelio walks back home, deflated, shoulders drooping. By now, the sun is starting to hide on the horizon. When he walks by the church, it glows like gold. Moments later, a skinny dog approaches and starts barking at him.

The Line

"What's wrong?" Rogelio asks.

"Get away, dog," Prematuro says.

"No, let him. He's trying to tell me something."

Rogelio pats the dog's head, and the animal lets out a small cry.

"You are hungry, aren't you? Did your owner leave town and leave you alone?"

The dog emits another cry.

"Do you want to come home with me? I don't have much, but I'll share what I have."

The dog wags his tail and follows Rogelio home.

Picture of Prematuro

Chapter 16

Matilda

(Amelia)

After a short drive, we arrive at Matilda's house. The driver drops us in front of her door, the only one on that block without iron bars. On either side of the narrow street stand a familiar series of row houses, each a one-story building that occupies most of the block. The building on the side where Matilda lives has a green exterior wall and decorative white columns that separate each house. Around the doors, elaborate carved woodwork speaks of their bygone elegance.

An elderly gentleman riding a bicycle passes by as we exit the car and greets us. I know him well. His name is Rogelio. His ordeal at the grocery store made rounds throughout Remedios when the *bodeguero* did not allow him to buy his quota of groceries for the month because the records showed that Rogelio had died.

When Rogelio notices me, he stops for a moment and says, "Prematuro was looking for you. He wants you to talk to the priest about dedicating a mass to his mother."

"Thank you for reminding me, Rogelio. I have been so busy that it escaped my mind. However, I promise I will talk to the priest tomorrow."

Matilda

Prematuro has reminded me a couple of times, and I keep forgetting. I feel awful.

Moments after we knock on the door, Matilda, a thin and wrinkled woman with short white hair combed back, opens and greets us with a friendly smile.

"What a nice surprise, Amelia. You haven't visited me in a long time. And I see that you have company."

"The gentleman needs to talk to you," I explain.

She glances at Frank for a moment and shrugs her shoulders.

"Let's go inside," Matilda replies.

After closing the door, she invites us to sit down on two old dark wood rocking chairs while she sits on another one across from us. She watches Frank with curiosity.

"You don't look like you are from here."

"I'm not. I live in Miami, but I'm here to inquire about my mother. My name is Frank."

"What a coincidence," Matilda replies. "My cousin Alicia had a son named Frank."

Frank stays silent, glancing at the tiled floor. Then his eyes meet Matilda's. I am still holding the food on my lap, but the time doesn't seem right for me to ask Matilda to let me use her refrigerator.

"Matilda," Frank says. "I'm Alicia's son."

Matilda covers her mouth in awe. "My God! It can't be. But how did you know to come here?"

"After looking for her for years, I finally connected through Facebook with people in this town who had known her. I didn't know she had returned here. When I left, she and my father lived in Havana.

65

Well, not exactly. He was taken to jail a few days before my departure. I was only a child back then. That is my last memory of him."

Matilda rises out of her chair with some difficulty and approaches Frank.

"Let me look at you, my love," she says. "Let me hug you, the hug my cousin waited for years to give you. Although I am your mother's distant cousin, here in Cuba, a cousin is a cousin. You can call me Tia Matilda."

Frank rises to his feet and embraces Matilda. Her thin body disappears in his embrace.

Frank's eyes fill with tears. He looks away from me and wipes his face. After a long silence, Matilda pulls her chair closer to him.

"Your mom prayed so much for you. The church said you had run away from the foster family where they assigned you. What happened?"

Frank inhales. "It's best not to talk about these things," he says.

"But I want to know. *She* wants to know. I feel that even though she's dead, her spirit never left. She is still waiting for her son, and she is here with us, so tell *us* what happened."

Frank's face has reddened. He nods and tries to keep his composure.

"My foster parents beat me, ridiculed me, and told me that my parents didn't want me. They treated their dog better than I did. I couldn't stay, so I left. At first, I didn't know what to do. One of my teachers felt sorry for me and let me stay with her. Afraid the family would want me back, I begged her not to alert the authorities. However, my foster mother came to the school looking for me. The teacher told her that she would report her to the authorities. She had pictures of my injuries. Mamá may have contacted the church after I ran away. In the end, the teacher adopted me. I didn't take anything with me when I left the house of my adopted parents. Any contact information I had stayed behind. The teacher tried to get my belongings back, but the family had discarded my things."

"Did the teacher contact the church to get your parents' address?"

"The church gave her the last known address. We both wrote to her several times. Eventually, the family who moved to my parents' house wrote back and said that my mother didn't live there anymore."

"After your father was killed, your mother felt lost. By then, the family she had in Havana had left, so she returned here. I had an extra room, so she stayed with me. She contacted the church to see if they could find your whereabouts. They said they didn't know. The last known address they had for you was your foster parents'. She wrote to them several times. They never replied."

Distraught, Frank sits on the rocking chair. He rubs his forehead and sighs. I feel like an intruder watching the exchange.

"Perhaps I should go back home and let you talk," I suggest.

"I'm sorry, Amelia. I didn't mean to take so much of your time. I can have my driver take you back."

"Oh, please, don't worry. It's not that far. I can walk home."

"Amelia, my granddaughter, wants to go to the Parranda on the 24th, and I will not let her go by herself. Why don't you and Frank come with us?"

"Tia Matilda, I'm in no mood," Frank says.

"Come on. Your mother loved going to the Parranda. It made her smile. She was a great dancer, you know."

"I do remember how much she and Dad loved to dance."

"That's what she told me. It was as if when the Parranda came to town, so did your father's ghost to dance with your mother."

"I guess everyone in this town believes in ghosts," Frank replies.

"They do exist. I feel the presence all the time. So, it's settled! Both of you are coming with us to the Parranda on the 24th."

"Tia Matilda, that's fine, but I was hoping to spend some time with you talking about my mother. I will drop Amelia off at home and come back if that's okay with you. Would you mind?" Frank asks.

Matilda nods.

"As you wish. I'll talk to my granddaughter."

Despite my insistence on walking, Frank had his driver take me home. He decides to accompany us. After the driver stops in front of my house, Frank escorts me to the front door.

"It would mean a lot if you came to lunch with me tomorrow," he says.

"I would love to, but I need to work. I was supposed to work today, but took the day off because I had to run some errands."

"Don't you take a break for lunch? We could go to a place nearby if you don't mind. This old man could use a friend."

I nod.

"You are not that old, but okay, Frank. I will let the priest know that I will need to take a longer lunch. I will be in front of the church at noon tomorrow."

"Which one of the two?"

"The biggest one."

"I'll be there. Thank you."

As it is customary in Cuba, I kiss Frank on the cheek, but he seems taken aback by it.

"I'm sorry. It's what we do. I forgot that you left as a child."

Frank smiles. "No worries."

"I'll see you tomorrow," I say before I open my front door and go inside.

Chapter 17

Mass

(Amelia)

Prematuro arrives at the church that morning wearing a bright yellow short-sleeve t-shirt, which contrasts with the conservative attire of the men in the congregation. Rogelio sits next to him. After so many years, he has become a father figure for the much younger man. Prematuro seems nervous, perhaps because I promised that today, the priest would dedicate mass to his mother.

For years, no one knew much about her because Prematuro didn't like sharing his feelings or many details about his life with others. A façade of happiness has long masked the sadness inside—until today. Prematuro's feelings surface as the priest begins the dedication. He traces the sign of the cross, his eyes downcast, and wipes away a tear. I heard from the priest that his mother had died the day before. Rogelio pats him on the back and whispers something to him.

Prematuro looks around the church; then, for a moment, his eyes focus on the Virgin, who looks up at the heavens with pleading eyes. The angst of the people in Remedios, of the mothers who have lost their children, reflects well in her expression.

Prematuro pays attention to the priest as he reads the Word of God. I can only imagine how he must feel, alone in the world, with no family other than strangers.

And for a moment, I feel wealthy.

Chapter 18

Frank's Story

(Amelia)

We go upstairs to the second floor of a colonial house that the owners converted into the paladar La Pirámide. The lunch crowd is starting to arrive, but luckily, we find a table in a corner near the rear counter. White linens cover the tables and chairs. Frank pulls a chair for me before we both sit down. Like the day before, I don't look at the menu.

"Why don't you order what you like?"

"Whatever you order is fine."

"I read they have good pizzas. Is that okay?"

My eyes light up. "That's perfect."

By the time the waiter returns with two tall glasses of water, Frank places the order.

"How's work?" he asks.

"Same as always. Uneventful."

I catch the scent of his musky cologne and notice his black polo shirt, adorned with a tiny red decoration on the left side. As if noticing my curiosity, he says, "It's a logo for Ralph Lauren, a man on a horse."

"I don't know much about logos, but it's a nice shirt."

"Thank you," he says.

Today, loneliness and melancholy color his expression. How can someone who has everything feel this way?

In the forty-five years I have been on this earth, other than my grandfather, I have never met anyone like Frank —so respectful and caring, an old-fashioned gentleman.

He apologizes for interrupting my day and my family. "It's no bother," I tell him. The curious part of me wants to know what he learned about his mother, but I refrain from asking him.

"I'm impressed with you and your family," he says. "I feel so much love when I walk into your living room. I miss those times when my children were young and my wife was alive. I felt invincible. It's different now. They live in other states. I have thought about moving closer to them, but I don't want to bother them."

"I couldn't live away from my mother and my uncle. If I don't make the lines and cook for them, they would not survive. Here we must stay together."

"What an unselfish and loving way to live. And what about you? What about your life?"

"I enjoy my nieces. They are the daughters I never had. I don't need much to be happy, but it would be nice not to have to deal with the lines and the blackouts, especially during the summer months." Before finishing my sentence, I get a little closer to Frank and whisper, "And the repression."

He sighs.

"I'm doing it again," I say. "I'm sorry."

"Please, it's fine. You can be yourself around me." He pauses. "I understand what is happening here. All the punishment in the world would not suffice to pay for what they have done. I have seen the pictures from before 1959. And now, the destruction... We always had fertile and productive farms. They destroyed it all."

"Some blame the embargo," I say.

A waiter comes over to bring our order. Frank waits for the young man to walk away before replying.

"The embargo doesn't stop Cuba from buying food from the United States or having productive farms like before. It just doesn't allow U.S. businesses to be established here on the island. Remember, Cuba had many American companies before 1959. However, all their assets were taken over by the government. Do you blame us for not repeating the mistakes of the past?"

I look around, hoping no one hears us. Snitches willing to report even their mothers could be anywhere. I cannot trust anyone.

"You are right. We should change the topic. Let's talk about what I learned yesterday. Do you mind?" Frank asks.

"That would be a safer subject."

"I'm not so sure. I was not expecting to learn what I did. Sometimes, it's best not to know."

"What happened?" I ask. "Now you are scaring me."

He rubs his face before responding.

"My mother had a very difficult life, but she didn't let life defeat her," he says in a low voice. "Matilda thinks dancing saved her. After *it* happened, she taught traditional Cuban dance to young people and even tourists. Every year, during the Parranda, she competed with other dancers. My aunt Matilda showed me some pictures of herself. She said she kept her sadness inside. She always carried my picture with her, hoping that one day I would find her. She never lost hope."

"It seems like you had an exceptional mother."

"I'm happy to know that she lived a full life. I wish she had remarried. Life is short, and it is meant to be shared. Unfortunately, she was destined to be alone and lost it all twice."

"I don't understand."

He remains silent for a moment and taps his fingers on the table.

"There is something Matilda told me that I was not expecting. It makes my blood boil when I think of it."

"What is it? I mean, if you feel comfortable telling me."

"It's difficult to repeat it," he replies.

"What is it?"

I take a bite of my pizza. The heavenly smell and flavor of melted cheese make me wish I could eat the entire personal pizza without saying one more word.

"When she came here, she wasn't alone."

I swallow, take a sip of water, and reply, "What do you mean?"

"My mother was pregnant."

"I don't understand. Wasn't your father dead by then?"

"He was."

"Then, what happened?"

Frank closes his fists tightly and then begins to tell me the story, stopping occasionally to grab a bite of his pizza.

His mother was a beautiful woman: tall with long brown hair and pale skin. "She looked like Rita Hayworth," he explains. "The same jawline, big eyes, and beautiful hair."

Frank explains that after the government jailed his father, an officer came to his mother's apartment and promised that he could save her husband with one condition. She needed to sleep with him. A woman of principles raised by Catholic nuns, she could not compromise her sense of morality. The officer, a few years older than his mother, tall and strong, threatened to kill her. At gunpoint, he forced her to go to her bedroom.

Frank pauses for a moment and eats the last bite before proceeding. His face reddens as he speaks.

The officer threw his mother on the bed and ordered her to undress. She was crying, begging him to let her go. He shoved a handkerchief inside her mouth so she couldn't scream and tied her hands. Then he forced himself on her.

Three months later, she learned she was pregnant. By then, Frank's father had been shot in front of a firing squad. Frank's mother arrived in Remedios a few months before giving birth to a daughter.

"What happened to the baby, your half-sister?"

"Your mother probably knew her. You are too young."

"Although I know many people in this town, I guess I don't *truly* know anyone."

"Not even those who live with us," Frank replies. "I have faced so many disappointments with my children." He pauses. "Anyhow, the records show that my father is also the father of my half-sister, Ana," Frank whispers as he looks around the half-empty cafeteria. "Only Tía Matilda and my mother knew the truth. Well, not exactly. That changed."

"What do you mean?"

"Ana always wondered why her skin was much darker than my parents'. You know children. They hear rumors at home, and the rumors spread. The children in her classes teased her and called her a bastard. When she turned sixteen, she begged my mother to tell her the truth. My mother had never been a good liar, and my sister looked right through her."

"What did she do when she found out?"

"She was furious and left town with Marcos, her twenty-year-old boyfriend, to find the man who raped my mother. Before my sister left, Mamá had given her his name. Armed with that information, she went to the police department of my parents' old neighborhood and reported him to the authorities. As expected, nothing was done. She was devastated."

"I can imagine... Poor girl. What happened next?"

"People in small towns talk a lot. My sister didn't want to return here. She also didn't want anything to do with her biological father for what he did or my mother for hiding the truth from her. She felt betrayed by everyone and decided to stay in Havana. Marcos and Ana moved in with his grandparents before their wedding and had a couple of children. The girl was the last one to be born when Ana was in her mid-forties. It surprised her. She didn't think she could have children anymore. She, her husband, and their son had been planning to escape from Cuba. They couldn't take the newborn with them, so they left her with Matilda."

"Did they make it to the United States?"

"Ana drowned," Frank explains.

"Dear God!"

"Ana's son delivered the message to Matilda through a friend. Marcos was never the same."

"What happened to him?"

"Marcos? We are not sure. The last time Matilda heard from him, he lived in Miami. This was a few years ago. He told Matilda that his father had moved to New York City. He has not heard from him since."

"Has Marcos' son seen his sister?"

"No, he hasn't. Not since she was an infant."

By the time he finishes the story, I consult my watch. It's already time to get back to work. After Frank pays the waiter, we exit the restaurant and start walking toward the church.

"Could I take you to dinner tonight?" he asks. "It would mean a lot to me. I feel I can tell you anything."

"I don't know, Frank. I feel like I'm taking advantage of you by accepting. I don't want you to keep paying for my food. You have done more than enough."

"It is you who has filled a void during my stay here. You are helping me more than you know."

"I don't know how."

"You are too young to understand, but loneliness has an ugly face, especially combined with the acknowledgment that the end is near. Now, you have your nieces and your family. Eventually, those you love the most will move on —then what? You must think about what will happen then."

"I cannot look that far ahead."

"You cannot love others if you are unable to love yourself."

"I get so overwhelmed with life. Who has the time?"

"You must find it ... before it is too late, and you ask yourself, 'Where have the years gone? What have I done with my life?"

We walk in silence the rest of the way while the people in town glance at us with curiosity. One of the older women, unable to resist her curiosity, stops and asks Frank, "Are you new in town?"

Frank is about to answer when I say, "He's a friend."

Frank doesn't say anything else, and the woman examines him from head to toe with suspicion. We then excuse ourselves and continue our stroll toward the church.

Chapter 19

Frank and His Niece

(Amelia)

Frank and I meet again for dinner at the Ebenezer Restaurant and encounter the same friendly service as before.

Throughout our meal—of pork, rice, black beans, and plantains—our conversation is pleasant, focusing on work, family, and ourselves.

"Have you always lived in Remedios?" he asks.

"Yes, I was born here," I say. "The only time I lived outside of Remedios was when I attended the University of Havana to become an attorney."

"I'm not sure what an attorney could do in a place like this."

I smirk and tuck my hair behind my ears.

"At the time, I was young and a bit idealistic."

He giggles. "That would explain it."

"So, I graduated and began to work for the government, not defending people as I had hoped, but in record-keeping." I pause for a moment and look around the restaurant. There is only a group of five people at a table on the opposite side of the room. Still accustomed to not speaking in public about how I feel, I whisper my next sentence while leaning toward Frank. "After access to the internet became more widespread, I wrote posts on my

Facebook page about the lack of food and medicine. I voiced my frustration at the ineptitude. More recently, even tourists, if they get sick, cannot find the medicine they need."

"I know. I brought some for different ailments in case something happens."

The waiter approaches us and retrieves the empty plates. As before, I have set aside half my meal and ask the young man for a box.

"I assume it's a yes to flan," Frank says, and I smile. After Frank orders two flans, the waiter walks away.

"So, you mentioned internet access. How do people on the island get access?" Frank asks.

"Through public hotspots. I read that approximately 70% of the island's residents now have access. But it is very limited. And restricted. Despite the restrictions, the internet opened the eyes of many people on the island."

I pause for a moment and look around me. Then, my focus returns to Frank. He glances at me with curiosity and holds his chin with his thumb and index finger.

"When I started to write my posts, I thought that by increasing awareness of the current situation, I could help my family and neighbors. Soon, I learned what a mistake that had been. The government blacklisted me." I shake my head with regret. "I can never work for them again. The government partially raised salaries to address rising prices, but people like me did not get a raise. The church pays me a fraction of what I could make working for the government. Therefore, food and the necessities of life have become unaffordable and inaccessible. I am glad my brother and his wife were smarter than I was and didn't dare criticize the government. Also, I am thankful for the help we are receiving from abroad."

"You're stuck because the government owns everything," Frank replies and sighs. "Do you have family abroad?"

"No, but a couple of years ago, on Good Friday, I posted a picture of my family on Facebook: the two girls and their parents and my mother and uncle with their walkers. We were getting ready to watch a religious program on television, and we were so happy that the government had allowed it to be broadcast. I took a picture of the family gathered around the television, even though I was a little embarrassed to show my house with its peeling walls on the internet. I did it anyway," I pause for a moment and take a sip of water. "The woman must have felt pity for us. Mayda, a Tampa resident, asked me for my address that night. I did not know why, but a few days later, we received a package of food. I cried when it arrived, thinking that God had sent us an angel to help us. That day, we all gathered around the table, my youngest niece carrying a cardboard sign she had written that read 'Thank you'. The food we received sat on the table. The kind woman has been helping us since then."

Frank inhales, and his eyes glisten. He looks away for a moment before responding.

"When I hear you talk about all your family is going through, I think about my mother. If only I had known how to find her. The Tampa woman is indeed kind. Unusual to find someone like her."

I inhale and look Frank in the eyes. "Let me ask you, Frank. Your mother sent you to the United States when you were a child to save you from this. Was it worth it?"

Frank looks down. He then rests his chin on his fingers and replies, "Life was difficult at first. I missed my parents. My old life was ripped away from me, and I was only a child. But after my adoption, acceptance kicked in. I was resentful of my parents for years. But now that I have returned and have witnessed the remnants... Now, I think my mother was a saint. It was she who convinced my father to let me go. And I am very thankful."

"What an unselfish act for a mother."

"They didn't have their visas yet. They couldn't leave at the same time. I had a visa waiver that she had secured through the Catholic Church."

"You were part of what became known as the Pedro Pan exodus."

"Exactly. Over 14,000 children left by themselves."

"I'm not a mother, but I am an aunt. I'm not sure if I could let my nieces go. If it were up to me, of course."

Frank glances at my hands. I'm embarrassed about my short and unkept nails and bend my fingers to hide them.

I glance down at my hands, acutely aware of my short, unkempt nails. Embarrassed by their appearance, I instinctively bend my fingers, trying to hide them from view.

"Have you ever been married?" he asks. "And please don't take my question the wrong way. I'm an old man who is not looking for any romantic pursuits. I'm just curious."

"No. Of course not. My family needs me," I respond. "My brother and his wife both work all day. My schedule at the church here in Remedios is more flexible than theirs. It's too much for them to care for their daughters and two elderly people."

"Amelia, you are still young. Life goes by so quickly. As a friend, I suggest you think a little more about yourself, or life will pass you by. You can choose to be happy."

"On this island, choices are made for us. If I don't care for my mother and uncle, make the long lines for them, take them to doctors' appointments, and accompany my nieces to their activities when their parents are at work, who will? That's my calling."

"You are an extraordinary person," Frank says.

"You are very kind," I say, and pause for a moment when the waiter returns with our flans. I take a couple of bites. It is so creamy and sweet, like a piece of paradise in my mouth. Frank giggles when he notices my joyful expression.

"I could eat this every day," I say. Then I think about my last conversation with Frank.

"So, tell me, Frank. What happened when you met your niece? Was she surprised to find you?"

Frank adjusts his glasses and shares the encounter with me.

***

Frank and His Niece

She arrived like a ray of sun, brightening the old, lackluster house. Smiling and full of energy, she dashed toward Matilda, ignoring the stranger who sat across from her grandmother.

"I miss you so much, mi abuelita," she told Matilda and pinched her cheeks. Matilda shook her head.

Frank stood up when he saw her, not believing his eyes, and brought his hand to his chest. "Is this my sister's daughter?" he asked Matilda.

The young girl was wearing white pants and a worn-out pink t-shirt.

"Hello!" she said to Frank. "You are not from this town, are you?"

Frank shook his head.

He noticed her dark eyes, the same eyes as his mother's. He had tried to erase the memories of the last time he saw them, tears streaming down his face. While standing at the Rancho Boyeros Airport in Havana, she promised that they would be together again soon. Frank believed her. His mother had never lied to him. But as the months passed and his life turned inside out, he lost hope. Years later, while he was in college, his wife—a rock of a woman—entered his life to help him heal. Twenty-four months later, his frequent nightmares ended. He felt safe at last. Now, this young girl had brought it all back from the precipice of his mind: the lack of belonging to the world, the loneliness, the sense of abandonment by everyone who ever knew him.

***

I sigh after Frank finishes his story.

85

"Sometimes it's better to leave the past in the past," I say.

"On the other hand, just because a wound is hidden doesn't mean it's not there. I needed to know what happened to my mother."

"You are looking for closure."

"I guess I am."

"What are you going to do? About your niece, I mean. Matilda is old. The day she dies, her granddaughter won't have anyone to care for her."

"I have been thinking about that. Matilda wants me to find her father and her brother."

"Life has given you a new purpose."

"More than I bargained for."

Frank and I continue to meet for lunch and dinner most days except the Saturday before Christmas. If I had known what was going to happen that day, I would have canceled the trip.

Chapter 20

Trip to Camajuaní

(Amelia)

The wind stirs my nieces' long, black hair as we stand on the back of the truck with other passengers picked up at Remedios. Mine is much shorter. I don't have time to care for long hair.

While the truck takes us through a long, winding road surrounded by lush greenery, scattered royal palm trees, and red soil, we hold on to each other to avoid falling.

I breathe in the dew-infused country air and listen to the chirping of birds, disturbed only by the sound of the truck's engine and casual conversations. Sunlight colors the green pastures and brightens the blue skies.

After a few minutes, we notice the familiar tall white sign to our right with the name "Camajuaní" in black letters. Andrea's eyes light up.

"Almost there!" she says. I nod.

A municipality and a town, Camajuaní is in a valley within sight of a leafy mountain range.

No one really knows where the name of this town originated. The most accepted version is that it is of Indigenous origin and means "clear waters."

In 1705, aboriginal communities had settled on the eastern bank of the Sagua La Chica River

87

near the cave of the Palenque Hills. However, the area did not experience the most significant boom until the mid-nineteenth century with the expansion of the sugar industry, which led to numerous mills being built in the region. The towers of the sugar mills that once brought prosperity to surrounding neighborhoods, such as Carmita, Fe, Vega Alta, and La Julia, are now in ruins. A few mills continue to operate at reduced rates. The sugar plantations of La Julia now handle all the local production for the harvest, but even they are in decline.

About 320 people work in La Julia Cooperative. Engineers are paid 5,000 pesos, and technicians are paid about 2,500 pesos (approximately $20 at the official exchange rate). Workers' pay is often delayed because the mills are heavily indebted to the Central Bank of Cuba. The industry is dying. No wonder sugar is so scarce. My nieces' wish list to the Reyes Magos includes one piece of chocolate and happiness for the family, wishes I will not be able to grant.

Ahead of us, two women walk in the opposite direction, each carrying a white plastic bag. They lift red soil in the air with their shoes as they walk.

"Can you buy me an ice cream when we get there?" Andrea asks me.

"We'll see," I say, thinking about the little money I am carrying.

When we arrive, the center of town appears busier than usual. A tractor goes down the street at a slow pace, upsetting the car driver behind it. A tricycle taxi going in the opposite direction carries an elderly woman. Men riding old bicycles travel in either direction. A thin dog tries to attract the attention of people walking by, only to be ignored. I buy some plantains from a street vendor. I don't want to carry it all day, but I'm afraid that if I don't buy it now, there won't be any left in a couple of hours when it's time to head back home.

Like Remedios, Camajuaní has started preparations for its own Parranda during the one time of year when this sleepy town awakens. On this day, the tall and colorful stage, taller than the tallest buildings in this town, is being built. In a few days, the streets will transform. The Afro-Cuban sounds of drums and trumpets, the statues and signs of frogs and goats, and caravans of people dancing to the music and chanting will roam the streets in celebration of the Parranda.

Simple people inhabit both Camajuaní and Remedios, the type who share the little they have with a stranger, the type who live and die, and no one will ever know they existed. They are family-oriented, kind, and caring. A friend of mine from Camajuaní told me about a local physician who had been caring for COVID-19 patients in the town of Caibarién back in 2020. Upon his return to Camajuaní, from the moment he stepped out of the yellow cab, people burst into applause and cheers.

Like in prior visits, elderly men and women greet us with "good mornings" as we walk by. Although the weather is pleasant, the girls say they are thirsty and ask me to go to La Casa del Dulce, which sometimes sells tasty but unaffordable desserts. Instead, I buy them one fruit drink to share. I take a sip of the bottle of water I keep in my purse.

We walk by the Park of Camajuaní, across the row of colorful colonial houses, and seek the refuge of a giant ceiba tree.

"Thank you for bringing us here today," Monica tells me, but when she glances at me, she must notice my condition.

"Tía Amelia, are you okay?"

I feel confused and anxious.

"I don't feel good," I reply.

I don't know what happens after that. Monica later explains that I fainted and started going into convulsions.

Accustomed to my attacks, Monica knew what to do. She dropped to her knees and placed me on my side as my body succumbed to the convulsions. Then, the sisters screamed for help. A man who was driving by stopped his truck on the side of the road and rushed over.

"My aunt is having seizures!" Monica yelled. "She has epilepsy."

"What do you need me to do?"

"We need to wait for her convulsions to end and take her to the hospital. When she fell, she hit her head."

He complied. The convulsions lasted four minutes, but I did not return to consciousness right away. So, the driver, Antonio, and two other men carried me to the back of his truck. The girls sat by my side.

It had been several months since my last seizure. They usually came when I was very stressed, but today, it took me by surprise. Maybe I had been worried about what Frank told me, about getting to the end of my life and realizing that I should have thought more about myself.

When I wake up, I find myself surrounded by the nurse, the girls, and Antonio. The girls explain what happened.

"My name is Antonio Castañeda Rodríguez," the man says. "You really scared me. I had never seen anyone with a seizure before."

"I'm sorry to have bothered you."

"Oh, it's no bother at all. I was going back to the farm when the girls called me. I couldn't leave them like that. They were so scared."

"Let me get the doctor," the nurse says. "I will be back shortly."

After the nurse is gone, I remember the plantains I had bought.

"Where are the plantains?"

"I have them on that chair," Monica says.

"I thought you'd died," Andrea says, and her lips turn into a frown as if she is going to cry. I grab her hand and squeeze it.

"I won't die for a long time, my love."

"Tia Amelia, what are we going to do now? How will we get back to Remedios?"

"Are you from Remedios?" Antonio asks.

"We are. Born and raised."

"Many years ago, my grandfather used to sell fruits and vegetables to a man by the name of Manuel. They were good friends. Did you know him?"

"I did," I reply.

"Are you serious?" Antonio asks. The tan-complexion man in his forties, wearing a generous smile, crosses his hands over his head. "Are you related to Manuel?"

"I'm his granddaughter, Amelia."

Antonio shakes his head. "Amazing!" he says.

"What a small world," I say. "If my grandfather were only here."

"I heard he was a great man."

"One of the most caring and loving men I have met. I am fortunate he was my grandfather."

A short silence follows. Antonio plays with the straw hat in his hand and glances at me shyly.

"Well, Ms. Amelia. If you don't mind, I would love to invite you and the girls to my humble home. It's nothing to brag about. It's in the middle of our small farm. I would like to share a ripe mamey with you and your nieces, if you're a fan of that kind of fruit. It's a good-sized one.."

"Mamey?" Monica says.

"What is that?" Andrea asks.

"It's brown outside and red inside. The sweetest fruit I have ever had," Monica replies.

"We could also have lunch. My mother is making ajiaco."

"I haven't had ajiaco in ages," I say.

"What is that?" Andrea asks.

"A delicious blend of vegetables, like yucca, sweet potatoes, plantains, and corn, with beef or chicken. Before adding all these ingredients to the pressure cooker, sauté the onions with garlic and tomato sauce. Finding and being able to afford all the ingredients nowadays is like winning the lottery."

"Well," Antonio says. "I don't know about winning the lottery. It hasn't been around in over 60 years. However, my mother is a fantastic cook, and

I guarantee you it will be the best one you have ever had."

"And your wife won't be upset if you bring so many people home to eat?"

Antonio looks down.

"She is not around anymore. She met a foreigner and left me."

"I'm so sorry about that."

"Ms. Amelia. I am a simple man. I haven't traveled. I never went to the university. The farm is all I know. I couldn't compete."

"Don't say that. So many women would be happy to have a good man like you in their lives."

"I have not met anyone whom I would be proud to bring home."

We stay silent. "So, would you and the girls accept my invitation? My mother would love to see all of you. Manuel was always very kind to her when he visited the farm to meet with my grandfather. Besides, we don't get too many visitors these days."

The girls look at me with pleading eyes but don't say anything.

"We can stop by for a little while. I am feeling much better now."

His eyes light up. "You won't regret it," he says.

"Now, we just have to wait for the doctor," I say.

But we don't have to wait long. The doctor and the nurse return moments later. He examines me.

"You probably had a concussion when you fell," the doctor says. "You must be careful. Stay hydrated."

"I will," I say.

Trip to Camajuaní

"If you have dizziness or any unusual symptoms, return to the clinic right away."

"I will," I reply. Moments later, the girls and I leave the clinic with Antonio.

Chapter 21

Antonio's Mother

(Amelia)

"Mami, I'm home," Antonio announces as we enter the small, modest house in the middle of a plantation field. The home is only accessible via a red-dirt road we took after leaving the main paved road, which is over half a mile away. I find the country house's thatch roof and polished cement floors, as well as the sweet aroma of ajiaco, comforting. All the windows are down, and despite the midday heat, the house feels cool inside.

The walls only display two pictures. I focus on one of them.

"It's my parents, shortly after their wedding," Antonio says.

"And the other picture is of you and your grandfather. I recognize him. You look so young."

"It has been a few years, but please, make yourself at home. Have a seat."

I pick one of the four rocking chairs in the small living room.

"Monica, you can sit there, and your sister can sit on my lap."

"I'll bring another chair," Antonio says.

He returns moments later with a chair and his mother. We stand up when we see her.

After placing the chair down, he introduces us to his mother, Onelia, then adds, "Mamá, do you recognize this young woman?"

Onelia adjusts her glasses and wipes her hands on the white apron she wears over her house dress.

"Her face is a little familiar, and look at those girls. They are so pretty! They look like three beautiful orchids!"

"Aww... You are very kind. Come on, girls. Hug Onelia," I tell my nieces.

They obey. Onelia embraces them and then caresses Andrea's face. Andrea glances at me shyly.

"It has been so long since the last time a child stepped into this house," Onelia says.

"Well, Mamá? Do you remember her?"

Onelia, in her sixties—with tanned skin and a wrinkled face—waves her hand in dismissal.

"I'm too old for quizzes! Just tell me who she is, and don't ask me so many questions."

Antonio chuckles.

"Genius and figure to the grave. That's my beloved Mamá. She doesn't change," he says. "Fine, then. I'll tell you. This is Manuel's granddaughter. Remember Manuel? The owner of the grocery store in Remedios. Grandpa's best friend!"

"Of course, I remember him!" she replies. "My father, Mauro, had very few friends, so that says a lot about Manuel. Now I see why your face seems so familiar. I can hardly believe you're his granddaughter! Where have the years gone? But please, don't just stand there like a plant. Sit down. Would you like some coffee?"

As much as I like coffee, I know how scarce it is, so I promptly reply, "No, thank you. I had a cup already." The last sentence is not true.

We all sit down and begin telling Onelia about my mother and my uncle. Not that there is much to say. They are home most of the time, watching life pass them by. We talk about my grandfather, his grocery store, and his boundless generosity. Onelia speaks about her husband, who passed away suddenly at the beginning of the pandemic.

"I miss him so much. I kept telling him he was working too hard and should take better care of himself, but he didn't listen. Now my son must do all the work, except for the few workers from town who come to help him every day. He can't pay them much, as you can imagine. My son works so many hours, from dawn to dusk. Thirty years working on this land... since he was a child."

"Since 1993?" I ask, remembering a story my grandfather had shared with me. The government nationalized Mauro's lands in the 1960s. Eventually, Onelia and her husband ended up owning a portion of the lands that the government had taken away.

"Yes, that's when we took over this land, but it did not look at all like it does now. Those in charge didn't know how to manage them, and most of the crops had died."

"That was during the 'Special Period.' The government distributed small parcels of land to farmers to try to increase production."

"That's right after they failed. However, for many, the Special Period has not ended. In a sense, we are luckier than most because we have food to eat. But we need to sell our product to state markets. If we have an excess, we can then sell it to private resellers. To have an excess, we must work very hard."

"It's a difficult life," I observe.

"That is. Farmers are the hardest-working people on this island."

"What's going to happen to this country?" I ask.

"I hear people say that we should fight to free Cuba. Some of my nephews did, and they ended up in jail. There are outside forces that want to ensure things don't change. Do you see how the Boinas Negras forces are dressed? Where did their weapons and uniforms come from?"

"There is a lot we don't know. In the meantime, we are in a limbo of world politics with no end in sight," I say.

We remain silent for a moment. Then, Onelia glances at the picture on the wall. "So, are you married?" she asks.

"Oh no! I have too many responsibilities with the family," I reply.

Antonio observes our interactions in silence. While his mother is talking, I notice him looking at me. We exchange glances for a moment, and he nervously looks the other way. His mother notices.

"So, Antonio, aren't you going to say anything?"

He chuckles.

"I was thinking about what you said," he replies.

"I said so many things. I haven't stopped talking in the last thirty minutes."

"About the orchids. Amelia, you do look like an orchid. Not only are they beautiful, but did you know that orchids have many uses in traditional medicine?"

"They do?" I ask.

"They bring order to thoughts and teach you to enjoy life. The Chinese also use it in color therapy."

"Color therapy?" I ask.

"Yes. This goes back to ancient China."

Onelia shakes her head.

"This son of mine," she says. "He's the hardest-working man I know, but his head is always in the clouds—ancient China. Come on! Is that what you were thinking about?"

He looks at his mother but doesn't respond.

"Anyhow, our visitors are hungry. It's lunchtime. Why don't you help me set the table?"

"Onelia, you really don't have to give us lunch. My sister-in-law is making lunch for us."

"Nonsense. You can have it for dinner. I will not allow a visitor of mine to leave my house hungry."

I smile.

"In that case, I'll help you," I reply. "If you allow me."

"Amelia, you need to rest," Antonio says. "I will help Mamá."

A few minutes later, we are all gathered around the table enjoying ajiaco, white rice, and slices of mamey. Onelia and I dominate the conversation. Antonio only says a few words, unlike when I saw him at the clinic. After a while, Onelia turns to my nieces.

"Well, girls, how's school?"

"Good," Andrea says. "I get better grades than my sister."

"That's not true," Monica says. "We both get good grades."

"That's wonderful," Onelia says. "Anything exciting happening these days that you want to tell me about?"

"My aunt Amelia has a boyfriend," Andrea says.

My eyes open wide. I wonder if my six-year-old niece has heard comments from people in town who have seen me with Frank. Antonio looks at me with disappointment.

"Andrea, Frank is not my boyfriend. He came to Remedios to learn more about his mother. We have become good friends. That's all. Where did you hear such a thing?"

"My friends at school," she says.

"Tell your friends that they are wrong. They should not be spreading rumors like that!"

"Don't mind them," Onelia says. "You know, children."

"It bothers me because I don't like being the subject of conversation around town. Frank is from the United States. He's an older gentleman. Good man. He is not looking for a wife, and I am not looking for a husband. I don't know why people in town must start rumors when they see a man and a woman enjoying a nice meal."

"That's small towns for you," Onelia replies. "Don't worry."

I'm visibly flustered about my niece's comments. I ask to use the restroom. I am overheating and fear that if I don't splash water on my face, I could start going into convulsions again. I spend a few minutes in the bathroom. After I return to the table, I feel better. Andrea gives me a guilty look. I glance at her in silence.

"I apologize, Onelia and Antonio," I say.

"No need," Onelia replies. "Children repeat what adults say."

"Maybe one of Andrea's friends heard something at home. It's so upsetting. I have been on my own since I was twenty—almost twenty-five years. The last thing on my mind is having a boyfriend. My time has passed."

"Don't say that," Onelia says. "Loneliness has an ugly face. I tell you from experience. These girls will grow up. They will not always be by your side. You need to think about that."

I remain in silence until Onelia asks, "Would anyone like some more food?"

"No, thank you," I say. "We ate more today than we have eaten in ages. So delicious. Thank you so much for your hospitality."

After the meal, Antonio drives us home. He doesn't say much along the way. To break the silence, I ask him questions about his parents and the farm. His answers are short and to the point.

When we arrive, I invite him in, but he tells me he has some errands to run. He assures me he will return some other day. I realize I had taken hours out of his busy day and don't insist.

"Thank you for everything," I say before he leaves. He smiles, nods, and drives away

Chapter 22

The Parranda 2022

(Amelia)

In two days, Frank, the stranger who came to this town and turned my life upside down, will leave. But tonight, for the first time in years, I am going to the Parranda. Frank, my nieces and their parents, and Matilda and her granddaughter Clarita are coming. A neighbor offered to care for my mother and my uncle while we were away.

I feel excited for the first time in years! But also nervous.

When night falls, we all leave my house on foot. As we walk, the sounds of music and the voices of the Parranda-goers grow stronger. The night is pleasant, not too hot, and the gentle wind brings me the essence of jasmine. We walk on the street. The sidewalk is too narrow for so many of us. Besides, there is no traffic at this hour. Not that there is much traffic here during normal days.

"Tia Amelia, you look so pretty in that pink dress," Andrea says. She and her sister wear matching dresses that their mother made for them, both light blue with wide straps.

I give her a quick hug and thank her.

Soon, we find ourselves in the main square surrounded by the crowd. Fireworks illuminate the night sky, and people dance in the streets to intoxicating music. Rum roams the street and infuses the air on this night of December 24th, 2022.

"¡Abuela Matilda!" Frank's niece yells so Matilda can hear her, despite the loud noise. "My friend is over there." She points in her direction. "I am going there to dance with her."

"Clarita, no! You need to stay with me here. If you want to dance, you will need to do it next to me."

"Please, let me. I can't ever do anything fun."

"Call your friend over. The two of you can dance next to your family. And that's final."

Clarita doesn't comply at first. Eventually, she stomps her feet, inhales, and signals to her friend to join her. Her friend, of the same age, joins us, and the two girls begin to dance while my nieces watch them and occasionally exchange glances. I can tell Monica feels like dancing by the subtle movements she makes.

"Frank!" Matilda says. "I can still see your mother dancing on these streets. I think she's here with us. If you close your eyes and let the music carry you, you will feel her presence like I do."

"I don't believe in ghosts," Frank replies.

"Try it! I insist. Open your mind to it. Close your eyes. Breathe in the night air. Immerse yourself in the music and the moment. You will sense her presence."

Frank shakes his head, but as if realizing that she will not give up, he obeys. We all watch him, except Clarita and her friend, who are still dancing. His eyes stayed closed longer than I expected. Then, the strangest thing happens. A gentle wind coming out of nowhere envelops us.

"Did you feel her?" Matilda asks.

Frank opens his eyes, crosses his arms, and rubs them with his hands.

"That gave me chills," he confesses.

"You felt her, didn't you?" Matilda says.

He looks at her, dumbfounded.

"Your mother has never left Remedios, Frank. She has always been here, waiting for your return."

The bright, colorful lights from the float, only feet away from us, allow me to see Frank's face. Moved with emotion, tears escaped from his eyes. I don't like to see a man cry, so I hug him.

"It's good to let it out, Frank," I tell him. "You have kept it all in for way too long."

He lets me embrace him. Matilda and my nieces also embrace him.

Suddenly, from among the crowd, I hear a voice.

"Amelia! Ms. Amelia."

I stop embracing Frank and look toward the voice. I see Prematuro wearing the same bright yellow shirt he wore during his mother's mass.

"I am so glad to see you here with your boyfriend," Prematuro says after he joins us. My nieces and their mother giggle and cover their mouths.

"Frank is not my boyfriend! He is a friend. How many times do I have to explain this?" I am yelling these words so he can hear me.

"No need to get upset, Ms. Amelia," he says. "I just came to thank you for my mother's mass. I didn't get to do it before."

"That's okay. I know you didn't mean anything bad."

"Well, so now that you don't have a boyfriend, can I dance with you?"

"No! I am not going to dance that way."

"These are the sounds of African drums, Spanish ancestors, and Taino Indians. This is the music from the sugar plantations: bongos, güiro, and maracas. Come on, Ms. Amelia. Let the spirits carry you."

Prematuro begins to dance. He lets the music drive his movements masterfully, commanding the attention of those around him.

"Come on, Ms. Amelia. Dance!"

My nieces and Frank encourage me to dance, and so do Clarita and her friend. I haven't danced since my twenties. I would watch dance programs on television when I was growing up and could move well to the rumba and African rhythms, but so many years have passed since then.

"Come on, Tia Amelia," Andrea says and moves in an uncoordinated fashion as usual. Her sister begins to dance as well and encourages me.

Finally, I begin to dance.

"You are so good!" Monica says. I laugh. Soon, all of us are dancing, even Matilda. I feel free letting my body move like this, so carefree, so unrestrained.

I look around, afraid people might recognize me. There are so many people here, many from out of town. I look up a few feet away and see a familiar face. Could it be? He is carrying a bouquet. They look like orchids, but what is he doing here? When he sees me dancing with Prematuro, he freezes in place. He then throws the flowers on the ground and disappears into the crowd.

Chapter 23

Another Year

(Amelia)

I am reviewing dozens of black-and-white photographs and newspaper clippings that my grandfather left me. My grandmother looks so elegant with her pearl necklace, black dress that reaches below her knees, and matching purse and heels. Abuelo Manuel wears his favorite guayabera shirt.

Cuba looked very different back then, with well-kept buildings and women who wore elegant dresses. True, we had another dictator in power, but according to my grandfather, who came from nothing and succeeded, life was much better back then.

Is this what the people fought for?

If my grandparents were to return to life, would they recognize this place? The breathless beauty of the green pastures, queen palm trees, and red soils of the countryside, along with the aqua-green waters that caress the white sands of our beaches, has not faded. But a veil of hopelessness covers our town, relieved only by the laughter of children and the unity of families.

Multiple generations share our homes. Their love for one another, God, and family has sustained us while we watch the destruction of our country.

The year 2022 is coming to an end. At midnight, all the adults toast with shots of rum to a happy New Year. Then, continuing the old tradition, I throw a bucket of water outside to take away all the bad things from 2022 and start anew.

Chapter 24

After He's Gone

(Amelia)

It is February 22, 2023. Over the past ten days, massive blackouts have extended from Matanzas to Santiago de Cuba, affecting four of those days, with the most recent occurring today from 3 p.m. to 10 p.m. We are lucky we have a gas stove and are able to eat. Other families are not as lucky.

It has been several weeks since Frank left, and life has returned to the same routine.

January 2023 marked the sixty-fourth anniversary of a group of bearded revolutionaries, with crucifixes hanging from their necks and promises of a better future, as they made their victorious entry into Havana, riding in Jeeps and trucks—their boots still covered with the clay-colored soil from the countryside.

My grandfather told me that the entire island turned into a giant Cuban flag, and cheerful crowds poured into the streets to celebrate. The dictator, Fulgencio Batista, had fled!

"This revolution is as green as palm trees," Fidel Castro announced.

But it would also be as red as blood.

Soon, the killings began, and a massive exodus ensued. If my grandfather had been able to leave then, I would have been born someplace else, away from towering palm trees and the most beautiful lands that "human eyes have ever seen," as Christopher Columbus said. That breathtaking paradise became my island jail.

Over 600,000 of my countrymen have left since the 1960s, including over 270,000 in the past year. Those of us who stayed don't have many choices.

I read the comments on Facebook. "They should fight for their freedom." "They are cowards for staying at home and not doing something." If only they knew what happened to those who lost their fear. If they knew about the bloodshed and the physical and psychological abuse that those who dared to stand up for freedom have endured.

On July 11, 2021, people took to the streets in mass to protest. But it didn't take long for those in charge to show them what they were capable of. Buses full of government men dressed in plain clothes and armed with sticks were deployed to Havana: cracked heads, bleeding faces, broken legs. Everything was fair game.

Then, the frightening, highly trained Boinas Negras —men dressed in black uniforms and armed to the teeth —and the rapid response brigades that seemed to emerge from Hell itself injected fear into the very soul of the island.

But that was only the beginning. In the days that followed, after analyzing hundreds of videos, police began to visit the neighborhoods and arrest some of the protestors.

Some never returned. Others faced such beatings that they became afraid of their shadows. We learned our lesson well.

So, when I read the comments on Facebook, I shake my head from side to side. If they could live one day in my shoes, I would show them the Committees of Defense of the Revolution, the police presence, the Black Berets, the screams that erupt from our jails, our reminders to live in silence.

Now, the silence has returned. But I must find a way to move on.

Frank left two days after Christmas. He wanted to spend New Year's Day with his family. I miss him, but I am glad I got to know him.

Frank and I have become Facebook friends. We communicate often. He tells me about his past travels to Finland, a place where the sun doesn't set all summer long—from early May to the end of August. He tells me about the brilliant lights of the Aurora Borealis. He shares with me stories about Paris, Madrid, Barcelona, Rome, and Venice, places I will never have the blessing of seeing. His tales and pictures invigorate me.

"Were you able to find your nephew and his father?" I ask him.

"Not yet."

"Matilda is sick," I tell him.

"I know. She told me last time I called her."

"What are you going to do if you don't find Clarita's brother and father?"

"I haven't decided yet. It's a big responsibility. If I had someone in my life, it would be different."

"Frank, I'm sorry to get involved. Don't you think it's time?"

"My wife will be the only woman in my life."

"Do you think she would want that life for you?"

"She wouldn't. She cared too much about me."

"Then, find someone."

"I'm not ready."

I decide not to insist. I have already said too much. I tell him I will pray to God for clarity. It surprises him that I care so much about his life and all the issues I must deal with.

"What about you?" he says. "When are you going to start taking care of yourself and finding somebody?"

"I'm too busy. You know that. I must make sure my nieces one day don't do what an eighteen-year-old from Santa Clara just did."

"What happened?"

I share the latest news with him. The girl was attending *the Escuela de Iniciación Deportiva Escolar (EIDE) Héctor Ruiz Pérez* in Villa Clara. According to the news report, she hid her pregnancy for nine months. She had no known mental issues, which made her actions even more appalling. At midnight, aided by a student and a school coordinator, she gave birth to an eight-pound baby boy. Sometime later, she threw him from the second floor. The baby died from his injuries.

The school and the government promised to initiate an investigation. The government always promises investigations, and nothing happens. How could a girl who plays sports hide her pregnancy for so long?

This is not the first event. In December 2022, a woman was arrested in Havana after the dead body of her newborn was found in the garbage. In November, a baby girl was abandoned in Artemisa.

The lack of contraceptives and the economic conditions are to blame, but something must be done. The government should have a way for mothers who are unable to keep their babies to give them up for adoption. Even if no one here in Cuba can adopt them, international adoptions could provide an avenue.

"It's awful to learn this with all the couples in this country who would give it all to have a baby," Frank replies.

"Now you see why my nieces need me. I don't want them to end up pregnant and feeling compelled to do the same."

He understands. I also share with Frank the letters my nieces wrote to the *Reyes Magos* (The Three Kings or Epiphany). They are like Santa Claus, except that in today's Cuba, children's wishes are simpler. In the letter they wrote this year, they both asked for a piece of chocolate. The woman from Tampa fulfilled that wish. She also sent us Spanish *turrones*, black beans, rice, coffee, powdered milk, and a much-needed liter of cooking oil.

"Andrea is so shy," I say to Frank via text. "I take her to play with other children, but even when she is in a group, she is within herself. So different than when she is at home. Here is a picture of her on an improvised slide, unlike the ones you have in the United States. This is not much of one: a piece of wood, rails, and tires on one end. Notice Andrea standing on the left of the picture. I need to help her get out of that shell."

"It will happen as she matures," Frank replies.

"Frank, I forgot to mention, I returned to Camajuaní the other day to buy some farm goods, and I saw Antonio, a farmer who had invited me to his house for lunch."

"I don't think you have shared that story with me before."

"Well, it was embarrassing. I had fallen and gone into convulsions. But anyhow, I think he likes me."

"That's good! How about you? Do you feel the same about him?"

"He is a good, hard-working man, but I don't know."

"Give him a chance. You never know."

I change the topic and focus on Matilda and Clarita. Then, it is time to return to my daily life. Things are changing in my life. I'm starting to enjoy these moments of conversation with someone outside my family, someone with whom I can be completely honest. It feels refreshing.

After He's Gone

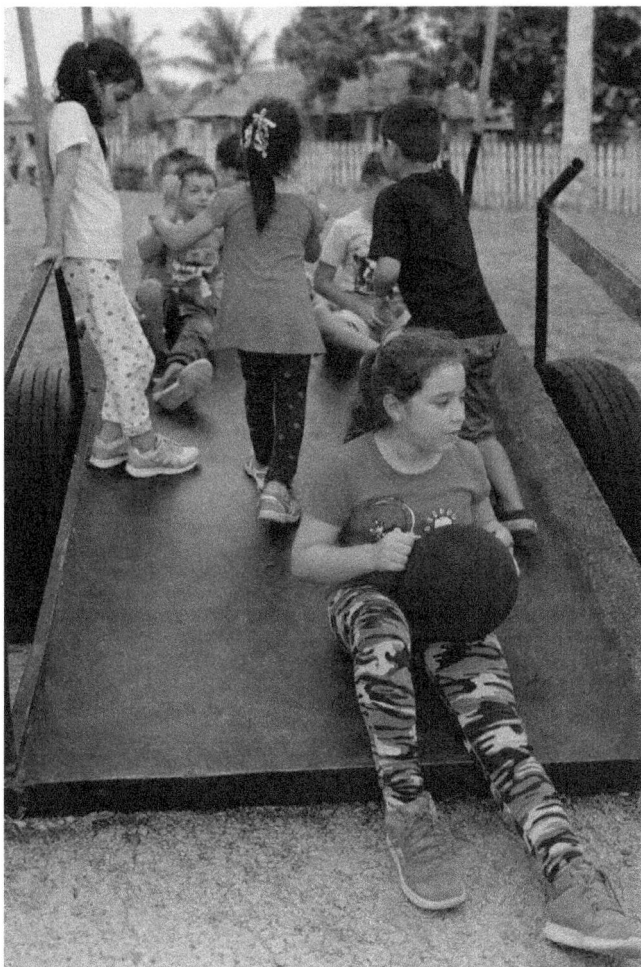

Chapter 25

A Grandmother's Cry

(Amelia)

It is Wednesday, March 29, 2022, a few days before Palm Sunday—the day when Christians celebrate the triumphant entry of Jesus Christ into Jerusalem. In the morning, I work at the church in Remedios, preparing for the Sunday processions. We are expecting a full church that day. As things become more difficult, more people in town have been drawn to Him.

A Grandmother's Cry

I take my lunch at noon. But instead of resting my eyes, I navigate Facebook, looking for something that catches my attention. I stop when I notice a video. For some reason, the woman's face in the video compels me to watch it.

Her name is Nilda Beatriz. From the start, her words shook me to the core of my being. The descendant of Africans speaks with her heart open wide. Her broken teeth, her saddened gaze, the emotions that roll down her face, and her words—so full of emotion—echo the screams of the Cuban people. She is Cuba in the flesh. I listen to her attentively:

I am sitting in my living room, very upset after my trip to the store. Six hundred pesos for a box of detergent! A pension is 1,500 a month, and the minimum wage is 2,100 a month.

How long? It is a joke, a lack of respect for the defenseless Cuban people. I am tired. Every day, my soul wakes up in a state of depression. I prefer to live like a beggar in the worst street of New York than under my roof, and I am not alone.

I was not supposed to look the way I do. But I owe my physical destruction to the totalitarian government that rules us.

I wake up and have no breakfast. The brain needs good food to function, not the fake ground beef that government stores sell. We want the foods that tourists and the country's leaders eat.

My agony is not new. It has lasted for years. I lost my job for speaking out against the government. There are no snacks or medicine for the children. How long, people of Cuba? How long?

A Grandmother's Cry

I have been hungry, so hungry that I have fainted in the street. I have bathed with detergent.

How long, Cuban people? How long?

Cubans have always had to invent. People abroad must buy food for their relatives on the island at very high prices. Why?

On Saturday, when I returned home, I had received an appointment to go vote. Don't they understand I don't vote? They know that I don't belong to any institution because all respond to the PCC (Cuban Communist Party).

I have tried to do the things they brainwashed me to do—to be kind and good and seek justice. But when I told the truth, I was shunted. I don't trust any of them. I cannot be an accomplice to evil. I am a Christian who recognizes her imperfections. I recognize my sins, especially when I read the Bible. However, if I allow evil and don't confront it, I am also a criminal, as José Martí said.

Yesterday, I saw an old man sitting in a park with a catheter connected to a plastic bottle that had been cut in half. He was peeing. A poor old man! I was on my way to finding a pair of shoes for my granddaughter. Why? I ask.

But he is not the only one. How can I help Pedro Dagoberto Valdivia, another old man who lives at a bus stop? He doesn't want to go to a nursing home. There is no love at those institutions, and when there is no love, there is no justice.

I'm tired! We are human beings with the dignity that God gave us because God himself is dignified.

How much longer will we have to endure this?

A Grandmother's Cry

I will stop now—too much pain. God bless you all. Share this post. I am on the side of light, not darkness. I will not support lies or the darkness. Only God can liberate us from the tyranny that has oppressed us since 1959.

I am Nilda Beatriz Alcántara Martínez.

I wipe the tears from my cheeks. I imagine the hell this woman lives in after deciding to start a war of words against those in charge, a war she may never win.

Chapter 26

Palm Sunday

(Amelia)

It is April 2, 2023. The town of Remedios has poured into the streets to join the procession on this Palm Sunday. Leading them are several priests, dressed in long white robes and adorned with a red cape. Deep blue skies contrast against the green palm trees on one side of the church on this sunny day. Nuns walk among the crowd, all celebrating the first day of the holy week, which marks Christ's entry into Jerusalem. My nieces and I join the procession while my brother and his wife care for my mother and my uncle. It feels good to walk the streets in support of our religion—a step in the right direction—but there is so much more to be done.

For over forty years, since the start of the revolution, processions like these would not have been possible. When Fidel Castro took over in 1959, he discouraged the practice of religion as he believed it contradicted the Marxist doctrine. Between 1959 and 1961, the government nationalized the property of the clergy, and over 80% of priests either left Cuba on their own or were forced to leave. In 1971, the Archdiocese of Havana reported only 7,000 baptisms. By 1991, that figure had increased to 33,569.

After the Soviet Union collapsed and its subsidies to Cuba ceased, the Cuban government altered its stance on religion. In 2008, Raúl Castro, Fidel Castro's brother, attended the official opening of the first Russian Orthodox Church in Cuba. Some believe that allowing religious practice is a means to an end. At least, I am glad that my nieces can believe in God without fear of ridicule. I see the difference between the children who have God in their lives and those who do not. During times like these, it is crucial to hold onto your faith.

After a short walk, I see him in the crowd. He is coming toward me with a bright smile on his face and a pot of orchids in his hand. We meet occasionally during my trips to Camajuaní when the girls and I sit on a park bench to rest. He will sit with us to talk about his farm, the weather, or his mother. He asks the girls about school and listens attentively to us as we speak.

During our first encounter after the night at the Parranda, he apologized for his behavior when he saw me at the park.

"I was jealous when I saw you dancing with another man. I had hoped that we could..." he glanced at the girls.

"Prematuro is a friend, and so is Frank. However, why would you be jealous?"

"I was hoping I could... you know. We are both lonely."

"I'm not lonely."

"Well, maybe not now, but you will be one day, and when you are, I want to be there."

"I have not dated anyone in over twenty years. My time has passed. Besides, I have obligations to my family."

"That is exactly what I find appealing. You are a decent woman. Not many women like you are left in this world, even fewer in this town."

We continued to meet casually, as friends, without commitment. Today, he looks different, dressed in an impeccable white shirt with black slacks, his full head of greyish hair combed back neatly.

"Ms. Amelia, these orchids are for you. Orchids for an orchid."

I smile.

"You are an unusual man, Antonio. Can you hold the orchids for me while we walk? I'm carrying this palm leaf."

"Of course. I'm not giving up," he says, then turning to the girls, he adds, "Can I borrow your aunt after the procession?"

The girls nod enthusiastically.

Palm Sunday

"They can't lend me to anyone! I make my own decisions!" I say, smiling as we walk.

A nun looks at me with a serious expression.

"We'd better leave this conversation for later. We can leave the girls and the orchids at home after the procession, and I can accompany you."

"You will make me the happiest man in Camajuaní. Thank you."

He walks next to me, happy like the morning sun, hopeful, as his purple orchids brighten my day.

Chapter 27

The Proposal

(Amelia)

Prematuro is passing by when he sees me getting into Antonio's old green truck. He signals his approval through his hand gestures and his smile. I move my head from side to side and wave at him. Prematuro never changes.

When Antonio closes my door, I hear the squeaky door hinge.

"I'm sorry about the noise," Antonio says.

"Don't worry. Where are you taking me?" I ask as he places the truck in drive.

"It's a surprise!" he tells me with a bright smile that reveals his coffee-stained teeth. His straw hat and tanned, strong arms make him look attractive.

"He is a real man," my mother had told me when she heard that he had met with me a few times during my visits to Camajuaní.

"Did you like the orchids I brought you?" he asks.

"They are beautiful!"

"I planted them myself. They have your beauty."

"You are always so kind."

The Proposal

"I don't lie. It's true. I almost forgot, are you hungry?"

"I haven't eaten lunch yet."

"Me neither. I brought cheese sandwiches to your mom and left a couple for us. I had put them in her fridge before I went to meet you. She gave me ours before we left the house. The cheese is from my cows. Mamá made the bread with our flour."

"Are they in the bag my mother handed to you before we left?"

"Yes!"

"What else are the two of you hiding?"

He laughs and hands me the bag. As he drives, he glances at me occasionally and begins to eat his sandwich. I take the first bite and close my eyes in pleasure as I savor the cheese's creamy texture and bursting flavor.

"Heavenly! You didn't have to do this. You are always so busy."

"Your expression was worth it. So, I guess you like it."

"I love it!"

"Drink some water. I brought two bottles."

"You have thought of everything, haven't you?" I say.

He nods enthusiastically.

Over forty minutes later, we arrive at Santa Clara.

"Where are you taking me?"

"You'll see," he replies and giggles.

"Does my mom know?"

"I'm not saying a thing."

When he stops near El Parque Vidal, my eyes fill with emotion.

"Did you know about my grandfather and this park?"

"I did."

"But?"

"I know this is your special place. That's why I wanted to bring you here."

He grabs me by the hand, and I let him. His glowing expression tells me how he feels.

Moments later, we sit under the shade of a Flamboyant tree on one of the benches where my grandfather and I used to sit.

He glances at me, takes both of my hands, and says, "I know you have responsibilities with your family and I with my farm. If I don't work hard, I don't eat. So, this is what I propose. I am lonely, as lonely as you will be one day when your mom and uncle are no longer here, and your nieces have lives of their own. I will wait for that day. But in the meantime, I don't want to miss the opportunity to have you in my life. If you can't stay at the farm because of your responsibilities, you can visit me on weekends. Everything can be done on your terms, but you will make me the happiest man in the world if you agree to share your life with me."

"But... that's not fair to you. We are always so busy."

"Life is not perfect. It won't ever be. So, what do you say?"

I look into his honey-colored eyes as he waits anxiously for my response.

Chapter 28

Clarita

(Amelia)

Loud knocks at the door wake me just after midnight.

By the time I reach the front room, my brother has already opened it. When I see the girl standing there—still in her nightgown, trembling, her face flooded with tears—I bring my hands to my chest.

"What happened?" I ask.

When she sees me, she pushes past my brother and throws her arms around me.

"It's Abuela Matilda," Clarita cries. "She won't wake up... and her body is cold."

I guide her inside, lowering my voice so we don't wake the neighbors. We sit in the dining room. I place a hand on her shoulder while my brother goes to the kitchen for water.

"Tell me what happened. She was fine yesterday when I saw her."

"We sleep in the same bed," she says, her voice shaking. "She went to sleep early, and I stayed up doing homework. When I finally went to bed, I had a nightmare and woke up."

She pauses, trying to steady her breath.

"She snores sometimes. Even when she doesn't, I can hear her breathing—it's louder than mine. But... I couldn't hear anything."

Her voice breaks.

"I got closer. I touched her... and she was cold. So cold. I ran. I didn't know what to do."

"Cold?" I ask gently.

"Like ice," she whispers. "And her skin... it looked different. Like she wasn't herself anymore."

By then, my mother had joined us.

"Her spirit has left her body," she says softly. "What you saw was only the shell."

I lower my gaze.

"Poor Matilda."

Clarita clutches my arm.

"What's going to happen to me?" she asks. "Please don't let them take me away. Tell them I can stay here. I don't want to be alone."

I glance at my brother. He understands immediately.

We barely have enough for ourselves.

By now, everyone in the house is awake. My nieces gather around Clarita, along with their parents, my mother, and my uncle. I remain beside her, trying to calm her.

"Frank was looking for your father and your brother," I say. "I don't know if he found them."

It's a lie.

He did find them—but they have families of their own now.

"Would you like to go live with your grand-uncle Frank in the United States?" I ask carefully.

She shakes her head.

"My friends are here."

"You would make new ones. It might be better for you."

"Abuela Matilda told me she would never leave me," she says. "Not even when she died. She said her spirit would always watch over me. If I go away... she won't be able to find me."

"Her spirit will go wherever you go," I say.

"This is the only place I know," she pleads. "Please let me stay."

"I could use another sister," Andrea says, stepping forward and hugging her.

"What about me?" Mónica adds.

Andrea shrugs. "What's wrong with two sisters?"

The adults exchange glances. Our eyes say what our voices cannot.

"I will contact Frank in the morning," I say. "He is your closest relative, and he should be part of this decision. For tonight, we'll find a place for you to sleep."

"We can push our beds together," Mónica suggests. "The three of us can sleep in one."

We agree.

We consider going to check on Matilda, but Clarita's certainty stops us. We decide to wait until morning.

That night, I barely sleep. I pray for guidance—and fear what will become of this child in a place like this.

***

The next day, we notify the authorities.

129

Clarita

I tell them Clarita is a distant relative, and they allow her to remain with us. Still, I must accompany the police to the house.

It is eerily quiet when we enter.

I lead them to the bedroom.

She lies there.

Still.

"She's gone," the officer says.

I make the sign of the cross and pray for her soul.

As I prepare to leave—knowing the government will take possession of the house—I turn to the officer.

"May I take a few photographs?" I ask. "For the girl. It's all she will have left."

"Nothing is supposed to leave this house," he replies.

"Please," I say. "She has lost everything. Let her keep something of her grandmother. I will also need to take her clothes."

He studies me for a moment.

Then he nods.

I brought two large bags. I fill them with Clarita's clothes and gather a few photographs.

When I step outside, I begin walking toward the church.

And I wonder what Frank will say.

Chapter 29

The Call

(Amelia)

"**I**s everything okay?" Frank asks when he answers my WhatsApp call."

"I'm sorry to bother you, but we must talk. Text messages won't do."

"What happened?"

I pause, not knowing how to phrase what I am about to say.

"It's about Matilda."

"Is she ill?"

"No. She... she went to sleep and never woke up."

"Oh no! That saint of a woman." He inhales and remains silent for a moment. "So, how is Clarita doing... after all this?"

"She's with us at home. She's scared. She didn't want the government to take her, so we lied and said we were related to her."

Frank takes a deep breath.

"That's not fair to you."

"Well, we'll do what we can, but that's not the main issue. She has nothing left here, Frank. No future, no family. I'm sorry to be so blunt, but her place is with you."

The Call

"I'm an old man. I will not know how to finish raising her."

"You will learn. You have extra rooms. You can give her the life that I wish I could give my nieces. It's time, Frank."

"I don't know what to say. I don't want to tell her that I found her father and her brother, but they didn't want to claim her."

"Then don't tell her. There's no need to discuss them, but please get her out of this place. Get her a visa."

"I'll see what I can do. In the meantime, I'll send you food regularly. It's not fair to take advantage of you."

"I won't say no. You know the situation here. The Tampa woman helps us, but there are too many of us."

There is something I want to discuss with him, but I don't.

"I'll wait to hear from you," I say and end the call.

132

Chapter 30

Goodbye

(Amelia)

Three months have passed since Matilda's death. Until now, Clarita has lived with us, but this is about to change.

"Clarita, my love, do you have everything?" I ask her as I comb her long hair.

"I'm not taking much, but I do."

"And the pictures?"

"I have them."

"If they try to take them away, beg if you must. Don't let them take them. Those are all the memories you will have."

"It doesn't make a difference. I loaded them on Facebook and sent them to Uncle Frank."

"I'm glad you did. When you get there, call me. I want to make sure you made it safely," I say.

"I will—no need to worry. I'm going to miss you very much, Tía Amelia," she says. That's what she began to call me after Matilda died.

Andrea hugs her and wipes the tears from her face.

Goodbye

"I'll be back to visit you," Clarita says.

"Don't say that," Monica replies. "No one comes back."

"Frank did," I reply.

"Over fifty years later," Monica says. "By then, many of us will be dead."

I open my eyes wide.

"I don't want anyone to die!" Andrea cries.

"Stop bothering your younger sister," my mother says. "No one is going to die, and it's true. Clarita will return to visit you."

Clarita turns toward me. She looks so pretty in the new pink dress that Frank sent her from the United States; it is a little big for her, but she will fill it out in no time once she can eat the foods that are luxuries to us.

"Are you sure Abuela Matilda will see me where I'm going?" Clarita asks me.

"She will, and so will your real grandmother and your mom. They will never leave you."

"Okay then. I believe you."

She embraces me tightly, and I kiss her head.

We all go outside, where the car waits to take her to Havana. The husband and wife in the car are friends with Clarita's father.

We watch her get into the car, and a strange feeling overwhelms me.

Will this be how I feel the day my nieces grow up and leave home?

Chapter 31

The Sacrament

(The Church)

Today, I dressed in festive colors to celebrate the occasion. Two lives will join in holy matri-
mony, but for me, this wedding has a special meaning, as the bride is one of our own, one of the angels
who roam this town and my halls, an angel who
needed a miracle.

My benches are full of people dressed in their
best attire, waiting for her to make an entrance.
Lively conversation animates my interior. Even the
priests and nuns seem more joyous than at other

times. I recognize many of the regular mass attendants like Andrea and Monica, who today wear white ribbons on their heads. Also, I notice some people I have not seen in a while, like the girls' grandmother and granduncle, Sara and Sandalio, who came in with their metal walkers. They have a hard time moving around, but today they are sitting on the first bench near the altar, wearing elegant attire. She wears a light blue dress with a pearl necklace, and he wears a long-sleeved guayabera.

Prematuro sits in the second row with Rogelio and Rogelio's wife on one side and a young brunette on the other. The young woman doesn't dress or act like a local. She wears a colorful, long dress and lots of jewelry, and has red, manicured nails.

But there are others here today, others that the congregation cannot see, like Manuel and Matilda. I feel their presence in every corner.

I never expected to see the bride married. She has lived as a nun, always caring for others. But people in town say that a stranger from the north came and changed her life.

The groom stands by the altar, waiting for his bride.

"Doesn't he look attractive in his grandfather's old suit?" his mother, Onelia, who is sitting by the aisle, asks one of the women in the congregation.

"He does. He looks so much like him."

Purple orchids and white ribbons decorate some of the front benches.

Today, so much light fills my interior despite last night's blackout, which makes me think of a Bible verse, John 8:12: Again, Jesus spoke to them, saying, "I am the light of the world. Whoever follows me will not walk in darkness but will have the light of life."

After a brief wait, the organist begins playing the standard wedding march. Everyone stands and looks toward the entrance. At last, the bride appears, wearing a white gown that Frank's daughter had worn on the day of her wedding, his gift to the bride. That is what I heard her mother tell someone in the congregation. The bride's brother, Hector, dressed in blue slacks and a white, long-sleeved shirt, walks her to the altar.

For the first time since the bride started coming here, she beams with cheerfulness. Her pink lips complement her fair skin and shoulder-length black hair, and she smells like a flower.

Amelia still needs to decide what to do after marriage and where to live: with her husband or her family. Should she split her time between Camajuaní and Remedios? Her mother and uncle want her to live her life. "It's time," they tell her.

As the priest speaks, the bride and groom smile, look into each other's eyes, and hold hands. The bride's mother wipes a happy tear. And for a moment, the congregation forgets about hunger, blackouts, and oppression. After the ceremony ends, people return home, and the silence returns.

No matter what the future holds, I will continue to stand here—like I have for hundreds of years—acting like a beacon of faith and hope and fighting darkness with light until the shadows that consume us are lifted from this island once and for all.

Epilogue

(Amelia)

Manuel, my ten-year-old, follows his father outside. The boy has learned from his father how to milk cows and keep pests away from the crops. Antonio also shows him how to fight. We are already in our mid-fifties, and the conditions on the island have not improved, even though the embargo has been lifted. So, crime is on the rise. We need someone who can defend us when we can no longer do it.

I never imagined that God would bestow such a gift upon me. My son was one of God's miracles. I asked God and the priest, "Why now, when life could not be any worse for the people of this town and this island?" And the priest replied, "Everything happens in God's time."

My son has filled my life with joy and sometimes with sadness. I love him as I have never loved anyone else, but with love comes pain and the fear that I will not always be able to protect him.

Onelia still lives with us. What a strong woman she is. She loves her grandson and sometimes spoils him too much. My mother and uncle died a year apart despite my best efforts to keep them healthy. Now, my old house looks so empty. Only Andrea, who just turned sixteen, and her parents live there.

Epilogue

Monica lives in Havana with a friend and her family. She graduated from the University of Havana with a degree in engineering, specializing in energy. She wants to do something to stop the blackouts, but she is also interested in politics. I ask her to be careful. She can't trust anyone. That's why she has surrounded herself with young Christians attending the university, some of whom are from our town.

While towns and cities outside Havana continue to embrace religion, Santeria is more prevalent in Havana. I hope that as more children who grew up attending church become adults and move to the capital, a change will be possible one day.

Frank continues to communicate with me through social media and letters. Clarita graduated with a master's degree in business administration a year early. Frank is glad that now that she is an adult, her father and her brother are much closer to her. Frank is still strong, but he doesn't want her to be alone, even though Frank's children treat Clarita as their younger sister.

As for me, I miss my mother and my uncle, as well as the life I had, but I have come to embrace my new life. I continue to participate in church activities and teach the next generation to believe in God.

Monica told me something the other day that validated the importance of God and religion to this nation that lost its way in 1959: "I have seen evil personified. I have felt the cruelty and intolerance against those of us who envision a different future for Cuba. Without the belief in God, without hope, the world and this island will continue to move toward destruction. We, the new generation, can't let it happen."

Epilogue

And when I heard her words, I knew that all my sacrifices, all the hours that I had spent with her, had not been in vain.

Testimonies

I had to share this on a Facebook post because of my frustration. I arrived at the bread store on April 17, 2023, and noticed a sign on the door that read, "Today, the bread will be sold by district." They say reality is stranger than fiction, and that is what we are facing here in Remedios. There are two ways to purchase bread. One is through the ration cards, but this bread emits an awful odor and is inedible. An alternative is the bread available at the Mypime bread stores, small companies I am not familiar with, although I suspect they might be owned by people connected to high-ranking officials. A loaf of bread costs sixty pesos there. Although the price is high, considering pensions of 1,500 pesos and a minimum wage of roughly 2,100 pesos, it is a better alternative. Now, this is not a possibility either. Committees of Defense of the Revolution (CDR) will have to collect money from the people in their district and then distribute up to two loaves of bread per household, provided they are available.

This is so disrespectful to the people of this town.

But this is not all; we have not had water in the faucets for a while. Additionally, the roof tank, where we collect rainwater, is empty due to the drought. Today, April 18, it is finally cloudy, and we expect rain. Hopefully, it will rain enough to fill our tanks. This is life in Remedios and other towns in Cuba.

Based on a post and communication with a resident from Remedios.

Karissa: A story of darkness and light

This is not a story about Cuba, but it is fitting to include it here, as it is a tale about transforming darkness into light. Karissa's mother wrote it.

***

It was a year ago that Karissa's dad, Greg, and I traveled to Lions Eye Institute for Transplant and Research (Lions World Vision Institute) to celebrate the annual Donate Life Flag Raising ceremony, where our daughter, Karissa, had been chosen as Donor of the Year. The memory of that most special day will always remain in our hearts.

At last year's ceremony, CEO Mr. Jason Woody spoke to us about the important work of the Institute's teams. He also spoke about the dash etched on the gravestones of those who have passed, reflecting the dates of their birth and passing. As he stated, it is a small dash, but we should not focus on the dates; rather, the dash represents all the days lived between them.

At the ceremony, Mr. James Rosa spoke of the over 80,000 recipients who received the gift of sight in 2022 through their eye bank's efforts. When I thought about all the people who had received the gift of sight in the past year and the years before, I realized that the dash did not end with the donor's passing.

Every time a cornea is received and processed for transplant by your Institute, you are handling a person's legacy, and their dash will continue through the recipients.

I would now like to share with you the story of my daughter's dash.

Karissa was born in Dunedin and raised in Florida. She considered herself an old soul. She loved old movies, old television shows, and music from the sixties. Her favorite band was the Beatles. She was very creative and loved to draw. Board games were always a favorite. No one could beat her at Scrabble. She could lay down a few tiles and net a triple-word score.

She was a very girly girl, loving makeup, nail polish, various hair and face products, and colorful clothes. However, her favorite items were purses and shoes. Her favorite flower was the Gerber daisy. I always gave her a huge bouquet of Gerber daisies on her birthday.

Looking back on her younger years, Karissa was so excited at age sixteen when it was time to get her driver's license. Sure, she was thrilled at the opportunity to drive the family car herself, but that was not the most important aspect of getting that driver's license.

Karissa had told us she very much wanted to be an organ donor. She felt strongly about this for years. When she was handed her new license, she was more excited about being designated an organ donor than about the license itself.

After high school, she attended college, earning her associate's degree and two bachelor's degrees from the University of South Florida in five years. She was excelling and enjoying classes at the university when our family's genetic syndrome started to interfere with her life. Unfortunately, the syndrome affected her health, and she had to forego her education.

Permanent disability soon followed before her 30th birthday. Even though Karissa was challenged physically, enduring forty surgeries in twenty years, her spirit remained bright. Prescription medications did not entirely relieve her daily pain. When asked how she was doing, she always answered cheerfully, "Hanging in there."

Karissa always had a kind word to say and often complimented strangers. It was just her nature.

An avid animal lover, she adored all our cats and dogs, as well as her shell family of tortoises and turtles. She was a loyal friend who would always give everyone a second chance. She was honest and had strong faith.

I am so proud that Karissa is my daughter. We were so close that we often joked that we were twins, 24 years apart. Two peas in a pod. She was the person I loved the most. We never ended our day without saying, "I Love You."

With both of us on permanent disability from our genetic syndrome, we lived together all her years, and we took care of each other.

It was the Christmas holiday season, Karissa's favorite time of year, and we were all ready to celebrate. All our decorations were displayed. Our presents were awaiting us, and we had planned a special holiday dinner. We hoped to finish decorating our tree with our whimsical ornaments that day and watch our favorite holiday movie, White

Christmas, in the evening, which was our annual tradition.

But it was not to be.

That Wednesday afternoon, Karissa passed away suddenly and unexpectedly in front of me from a pulmonary embolism. It was December 23, 2020, just two days before Christmas. She was only forty. I did not realize she had passed away when the paramedics rushed her from our home to the hospital. Greg and I rushed to the hospital from our respective homes, praying she would be all right. We later learned at the hospital that she did not have a heartbeat from the time the paramedics took her from our home.

We asked immediately about organ donation in the emergency room, but the doctor shared with us that too much time had passed. It saddened us that Karissa's final gift was not to be realized. I have never known such grief. I had lost my parents and other relatives, but this grief was nothing like those other deaths.

Then we had to plan her funeral. Over the years, through many conversations, Karissa shared with me what she wanted for her funeral. Of course, I remembered every detail she shared with me, but I couldn't imagine I would ever need to know this information, certain that I would pass away before her. That was not the right order of things.

Greg and I spent Christmas Eve at the funeral home planning the "arrangements." Instead of our usual fun activities on Christmas Eve, we were choosing her casket.

A quiet Christmas day followed, and the next day, we were at the cemetery, choosing her final resting place. I was numb, in shock, and in disbelief. Everything was a fog. I was going through the motions with crippling and constant grief. I kept hoping that when I got home, she would be right there on the sofa waiting for me.

I will never forget Wednesday, December 29, 2020. It was mid-morning, and I had received several more floral bouquets. I took them to the funeral home, and when I returned home, I found I had received a voicemail. This message would change our lives.

The call was from Janine at Lions Eye. She needed me to return her call as soon as possible. I called back immediately. Janine was so nice. First, she extended her condolences to Karissa's family over her passing. I couldn't help but wonder, how does she know about my daughter? Then, she explained the reason for her call. She stated that after Greg and I had left Karissa's hospital room at her passing, their transplant team went in and was able to harvest both of Karissa's corneas. I was so shocked at what I heard that I began to weep openly on the phone. Now, I learned that Karissa's final wish had been accomplished.

We spent the next few hours reviewing Karissa's complete medical history.

Janine confirmed that, based on everything I had shared, Karissa's corneas would be transplanted internationally into two people. These individuals would gain sight through Karissa's donation. She told me I could check back with her in mid-February and that she would share limited information.

During Karissa's adult years, she often felt discouraged by her disability, but now she has the opportunity to change someone's life in a profoundly meaningful way. I find it difficult to express how this profound gift made me feel. I was so devastated by her death, but now it has a special meaning. She would live with two people. Two people would see the world through her very eyes.

The darkest moment of my life had turned into light.

Having learned this information, both Greg and I felt differently about Karissa's passing. Even though Karissa was disabled, she, in her final moment, was finally able. Her final wish was going to be realized. This transformed our grief, knowing how important this was to our daughter.

On Thursday, December 30th, we attended Karissa's memorial service. Due to COVID, Greg and I were the only ones allowed to be present. Everything was as she had wished. Karissa wanted only four things for her funeral. She wanted to be buried at Sylvan Abbey Cemetery, where all our family members are resting. She wanted to be buried in her pajamas, just like her grandma. I selected her favorite purple owl pajamas and my fluffy white socks, the ones she loved best. She wanted all our pets who had passed before her to be tucked in beside her. Every one of our kitties and dogs' urns was surrounding her body. Lastly, there was her final wish. Many years ago, when she was a tender age, Karissa shared with me that she wanted only one song played at her funeral. She told me she wanted "What a Wonderful World" by Louis Armstrong to be that one special song.

Karissa and I always felt that the song was from the perspective of someone who had already passed away, looking back on the world.

When I thought about her corneas being harvested, I knew it was not by chance that that very song was the one she chose. The song describes all the wonders of the world he sees through his own eyes.

Now, two people were going to have sight because of Karissa. I knew the song choice was not a coincidence; it was meant to be. "What a Wonderful World" was played at the beginning and again at the end of her service as we said our final goodbyes.

Greg and I each chose something special as a final remembrance for Karissa.

I chose Gerber daisies of all colors to adorn her casket. No other flower would do.

Greg chose her favorite childhood stuffed bear, Brownie, who had been with her through many of her medical struggles. He was old and worn, with patches of fur missing where she had loved the fur right off him. Greg placed her beloved Brownie over her heart as we gave our final kisses and said goodbye to our precious Karissa.

I could not wait until February to learn who the recipients were. It was the only thing I was holding onto. The grief of losing Karissa never lessened. She is the first thought I have each morning and the last thought each night.

February finally came, and Janine shared with me that Karissa's corneas had been transplanted to Jordan and that the surgeries had been successful. I felt, with all my heart, that her recipients were both girls, and I got the tingly feeling I

149

always get when I know Karissa is nearby. I asked if I could write a letter to the recipients, and Janine said I could. Now, I had a purpose for getting up each day. I wanted her two recipients to know who Karissa was, what she loved, and what was important to her, and to really know her. The only way I could think of doing this was to write her life story. I started writing my letter on the first of March in 2021. When the story was finished in September, I knew I had to do more.

I decided that I wanted her recipients to not only read about Karissa but also to see her in photographs. It was now October of 2021: 91 pages of text had been written, and 187 pages of photographs remained. The letter was now a book, five inches high, in a huge binder, with my favorite picture of Karissa on the front cover, taken at age 3.

Along with the two recipients, I made an extra copy of the book for the Lions Transplant Institute. Knowing that they dealt with corneal tissue every day, I also wanted them to know the person behind Karissa's corneal tissue.

I wanted her recipients to be able to answer, should anyone ask them, "Do you know your donor? With a resounding, "Yes, let me tell you all about a woman named Karissa, " Greg and I drove the "letters" over to Destiny, with whom I had been speaking over the summer at the Institute. Destiny shared that the two recipients were indeed girls. One was twenty-seven, and one was just five. Both had restored sight for life from Karissa's corneas.

James Rosa volunteered to read my letters and advised me on the day they were mailed to Karissa's recipients in Jordan. James later called me on December 22, 2021, and told me that the recipients had received my letters that very day. The next day was the first anniversary of Karissa's Heaven Day.

I must pause and say that each of the people with whom I worked at the Institute, Janine, Destiny, and James, always extended every kindness to me. They listened with their hearts and always gave comforting words. They never hurried our conversations. They listened, which is not an easy task when emotions are running high and tears are flowing. On March 4th of last year, Karissa was honored as the Donor of the Year at the annual Donate Life Flag Raising celebration. Greg and I, along with Karissa's best friend Dana, went to the ceremony. I was asked to say a few words about Karissa, and James had arranged for a large, framed photograph of Karissa to be displayed at the ceremony. I was so proud to tell everyone about Karissa, her accomplishments, her character, the whimsical things she loved, and, of course, my deep love for my daughter. My voice caught several times, and tears were brimming, but I forced myself to keep going, even when the words were difficult to say and caught in my throat.

Following the ceremony, the most unexpected miracle happened. We all went inside, and James presented to us large, framed photographs of Karissa's two recipients. This was the first time in the history of the Institute that any foreign recipient had ever responded to the Institute or a donor family. When James revealed the photographs, everyone gasped. I advanced to the photographs, and emotions overtook me. I was in awe of seeing Karissa's two recipients.

There they were, in the photographs, simply beautiful. I was immediately drawn to their eyes, just staring at them, realizing they were looking back at me through Karissa's own eyes—such a profound moment. And we learned their names. Rana was now 28 years of age and the mother of two small children. Izdehar was now six.

We received photographs of Rana with her little boy sitting on her lap and of Izdehar with her mother. Her mother's face is the most exuberant face of joy I have ever seen. We learned that Izdehar and her mother are Syrian refugees taking shelter in Jordan. Rana and Izdehar were holding my letter open, showing Karissa's pictures. I wept, as I believe all of us did on that most special of days. All of us felt at peace and at one, and we were connected in that moment. Karissa's final wish did come true, and I know she lives on in both Rana and Izdehar.

I know in my heart that, one day, Karissa and I will be together again forever.

Each Friday afternoon, Greg and I bring fresh flowers to our daughter and visit her at her resting place. Etched in her marker is her dash. Through her corneal donation, Karissa's dash continues in the lives of Rana and little Izdehar. Their photographs now hang on the walls in the memorial area I have in my home for Karissa. I see my new family members and photographs of the Lions Institute and Jordan Eye Bank teams every day. The circle of photographs is now complete with photos of Karissa, the two skilled and talented eye bank teams, and her two recipients. Her legacy continues throughout their lives. What a miraculous blessing to behold.

Testimonies

Written by Janine Funk, Karissa's Mom.

The work of the Lions Eye Institute for Transplant and Research (Lions World Vision Institute) is made possible through the generosity of its supporters. When you make a gift to the Lions Eye Institute Foundation, you support cutting-edge ocular research, sight restoration, surgeon training, vision screenings, and so much more. If you would like to support its mission, please send your contributions to the Lions Eye Institute Foundation with "Re: Karissa's story" in the subject line.

Address: 1410 N. 21st St.
Tampa, FL 33605

(813) 289-1200

Acknowledgments

Conchita Hicks, for being a fantastic beta reader and providing valuable recommendations.

Desiree Gonzalez, for providing insightful information about her faith in God and contributing to changes in the last chapter.

Susana Mueller, from Susanabooks, for designing a superb book cover and for being a beta reader for this manuscript.

Katherine Lima, for her story about her grandfather and the stories she has shared with me about her family, which inspired this novel.

Nilda Beatriz Alcántara Martínez, the Cuban grandmother of African roots, who allowed me to use her testimony and picture. She wants the world to know what is happening on the island.

To those who uploaded videos about Remedios on YouTube, which helped visualize the town.

To the Facebook group *All Things Cuban* for providing an important forum for the dissemination of Cuban history and culture.

To the Facebook group *Women Reading Great Books* for providing an important outlet for authors and readers.

Acknowledgments

To my husband Ivan, for making suggestions about various chapters of this book. His contributions have been invaluable.

To my mother-in-law, Madeline, and my sister, Lissette, for their contributions.

To all the readers who continue to support me and share my posts, and to all the book clubs that have selected my books, too many to mention.

To the writers of the following articles:

Las Parrandas de Remedios: Bright Lights Shine in Cuba's Oldest Festival | Travel| Smithsonian Magazine

The Mysterious History of the Vampire of San Juan de los Remedios in Cuba (ashepamicuba.com)

Reports from Cuba: Sugarcane workers barely surviving in Camajuaní, Cuba – Babalú Blog (babalublog.com)

Las Parrandas: Navidades a la cubana - BBC News Mundo

About the Author

Betty Viamontes was born in Havana, Cuba. At age fifteen, Betty and her family crossed the Florida Straits in an overcrowded shrimp boat on a stormy night when many families perished. This trip would reunite the family with Betty's father in the United States after almost twelve years of separation. Betty Viamontes completed graduate studies at the University of South Florida. Upon her mother's death, Betty dedicated her life to capturing the stories of people without a voice. Her stories have traveled the world, from the award-winning *Waiting on Zapote Street* to the No. 1 new release, *The Girl from White Creek*.

Other works include:
Havana: A Son's Journey Home
The Dance of the Rose
Candela's Secrets and Other Havana Stories
Flight of the Tocororo (Collaboration)
Brothers: A Pedro Pan Story (Awarded Best Fiction 2022)
Seeking Closure: The Pedro Pan Girls
Love Letters from Cuba
Crossing North: Tribulations of a Cuban Doctor

About the Author

The above books are available in English and Spanish. Waiting on Zapote Street was one of the winners of The Latino Books Into Movies award and has been selected by a United Nations women's book club and many others.

Her works have appeared in various publications, including the prestigious literary journal The Mailer Review.

www.ingramcontent.com/pod-product-compliance
Lightning Source LLC
Chambersburg PA
CBHW051828040426
42447CB00006B/420